BREAST CANCER

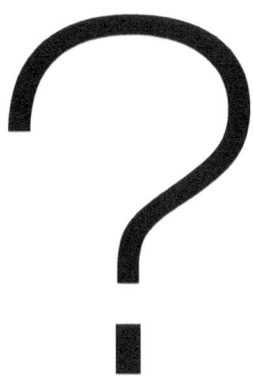

*My Journey from Suspicious
Mass to Five Years Cancer-Free*

ANDREA K. LONG

BALBOA
PRESS

A DIVISION OF HAY HOUSE

Balboa Press books may be ordered through booksellers or by contacting:

Balboa Press
A Division of Hay House
1663 Liberty Drive
Bloomington, IN 47403
www.balboapress.com
1 (877) 407-4847

Because of the dynamic nature of the Internet, any web addresses or
links contained in this book may have changed since publication and
may no longer be valid. The views expressed in this work are solely those
of the author and do not necessarily reflect the views of the publisher,
and the publisher hereby disclaims any responsibility for them.

The author of this book does not dispense medical advice or prescribe
the use of any technique as a form of treatment for physical, emotional,
or medical problems without the advice of a physician, either directly
or indirectly. The intent of the author is only to offer information
of a general nature to help you in your quest for emotional and
spiritual well-being. In the event you use any of the information in
this book for yourself, which is your constitutional right, the author
and the publisher assume no responsibility for your actions.

Any people depicted in stock imagery provided by Thinkstock are
models, and such images are being used for illustrative purposes only.
Certain stock imagery © Thinkstock.

Print information available on the last page.

ISBN: 978-1-5043-7314-2 (sc)
ISBN: 978-1-5043-7315-9 (hc)
ISBN: 978-1-5043-7320-3 (e)

Library of Congress Control Number: 2017900584

Balboa Press rev. date: 01/30/2017

PREFACE

"What you find in your mind is what you put there.
Put good things in there."
Ron Rathbun

If you or someone you know has been diagnosed with <u>breast cancer</u>* this is a book that will be helpful. This is my story from the discovery of the "suspicious" mass in a routine yearly <u>mammogram</u> to the present.

I wish I had had this book available to me when I began my breast cancer journey. Instead I spent hundreds of hours and thousands of dollars trying to discover the information that **I** needed in order to make the best possible decisions for **my** treatment and care.

The intent of this book is to provide information in a clear and concise manner. If you want to know some of the facts - some of the options that others have tried - this book will be of help.

Breast Cancer? is a collection of information from mainstream, conventional (<u>Allopathic</u>) Western Physicians, from <u>Holistic</u> (a combination of <u>Complementary</u> and

---

* The underlined words are defined in the Glossary. These were new words added to my vocabulary during my journey.

<u>Alternative</u> ideas) medical providers and from <u>Integrative</u> (using a combination of Western and Holistic Medical practices) medical practioners.

If you do not have the energy to read through all of this information go to the end of each chapter and read the bulleted items for suggestions **I** found helpful for **my journey**.

I am just an average consumer who is now considered to be cancer free 5 years after my breast cancer diagnosis/treatment.

This book is not a substitute for professional medical counseling; it is meant for informational purposes only. Each diagnosis/case is unique. Consult your medical provider before using any of the ideas contained in these pages.

THANK YOU!!!!!!

A HUGE THANK YOU to the following: Dr. Jimenez, my Surgeon, who was willing to do what I asked; Dr. Browne, my Oncologist, from whom I felt love and support even when I did not follow all of her medical advice; to the staff at Southern New Hampshire Medical Center, who made a very scary situation less scary by explaining everything that was being done and doing so with humor and compassion; to everyone (especially the patient dog – Bailey) at the Southern New Hampshire Radiation Center for their welcoming smiles (and tail wagging), their understanding and humor; to everyone who read these pages especially Patty Schmidt (who spent hours editing), Lyn Walfish (a cancer survivor for her invaluable comments), Bill McLeod (for proofreading), Lois Wisman, Erika Scheschareg, Marcy Abbott and Alan Mulak for their encouragement and especially to my husband, Doug, who lived through this entire experience with me.

To all of the above I give much gratitude for their help in offering this gift to any woman who is starting on this long, frightening path. If I have helped one woman to have an easier time than I had with a breast cancer diagnosis the effort will have been more than worth it.

MOST SINCERE BEST WISHES
Andrea

Disclaimer: I consulted many professionals, books, pamphlets and websites to obtain information. I have made every effort to include my sources. If any source has been omitted it is unintentional.

CHAPTER 1

Surgeon #1

Emerson suggests we make our way on our respective trails,
not paths - so we don't just follow along where others have trod.

My first thought upon seeing the <u>mammogram</u> and <u>ultrasound</u>
was – If this is NOT <u>cancer</u> I'll be shocked. The mass LOOKED
like what I thought a cancerous <u>tumor</u> would look like.

My second thought was – I need to pay close attention to
what I am experiencing from now on. I am entering a world
that is totally foreign to me. This will be one of the most
important journeys of my lifetime.

Little did I know that the recall I had received after my
original mammogram was really for a <u>diagnostic mammogram</u>
and that having an ultrasound was not part of a usual process.
I had not given much thought to this recall since it had been
posted in several places in the Mammography Center that
it was often necessary to have additional images and it was
nothing to worry about. I had been told the same thing by
the woman who scheduled the recall appointment so I didn't
worry.

However, I did begin to worry when the lab tech doing the
ultrasound casually mentioned that she was attempting to see

what was behind "the mass". Up until that moment I didn't know there was "a mass" to look behind.

I had never seen a <u>radiologist</u> after a mammogram but this time I was told I needed to speak with Dr. X, the radiologist. I was now pretty sure that the comment by the tech was correct and that there was a problem. Waiting alone for over 5 minutes in a corridor (without even a chair to sit in) didn't help my mental state; in fact I seriously considered bolting out the door.

Once I calmed myself I decided to stay to hear what the radiologist had to say. She showed me the diagnostic mammograms and ultrasound and used the word "suspicious" as she pointed out the areas of concern. The mass had very irregular edges, which to me meant cancer. The <u>calcifications</u> were newly seen and clustered. I had no idea what those meant. She handed me the business cards of two <u>surgeons</u> - both female - who had offices near where I live and suggested I contact one of them as soon as possible. There was no statement of "I'm sorry to have to give you this news". There was no asking if there was anyone I wanted to call while still in her office. There was no inquiry as to where I might be going after leaving her office. In fact she never got out of her chair and didn't even walk me to the door of her office or point the way out of the building. As I exited the waiting room I imagined that everyone was looking at me and thinking, "Oh, the poor dear, she has just been told she has breast cancer."

When I arrived home I told my husband that I thought the radiologist had just told me that I had breast cancer – though she had not used those words. I told him what I had seen on the monitor.

I called the office of one of the surgeons and made an appointment for the following week. When asked why I was making the appointment I told receptionist that I had just been told that the results of my mammogram indicated "a suspicious mass".

Several days later I received a letter from the radiologist in which she explained the findings of the recent diagnostic mammogram. The words "mass suspicious for <u>malignancy</u>" were clearly written. The size of the mass was stated in mm (<u>millimeters</u>). If the radiologist had originally said the word malignancy I did not hear it. I did not know how big this mass was since I had never bothered to learn metric measurement but it sounded big. Why don't they write the numbers in inches? Inches would have sounded less frightening.

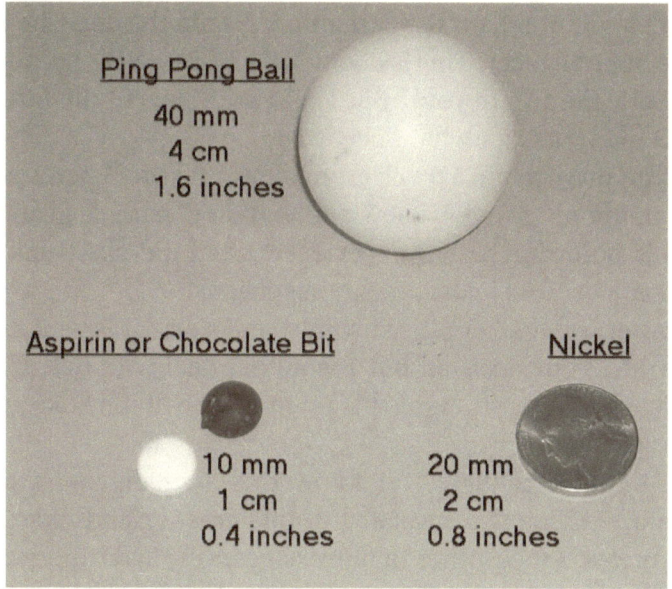

mm, cm, inches

Within a week I was sitting in a surgeon's office. I had asked my husband to accompany me, to take notes and ask any questions he had including ones I may not have considered. (I am fortunate to have a husband who can be concerned and pragmatic.)

The surgeon explained the information she had. She then recommended that I have the suspicious areas <u>biopsied</u>. She used the words<u>: diagnostic procedures,</u> <u>cone (or was it core)</u>

biopsy, needle biopsy, stereotactic biopsy, DCIS, Ductal Carcinoma in Situ, Intraductal Carcinoma, calcifications, infiltration, duct, encapsulated, IDC, Infiltrating Ductal Carcinoma, lesion, nonmalignant, benign, cyst and I'm sure other words that I missed.

When we started asking her what those words meant she explained them with equally unknown words. When my husband asked for further explanations she replied that she had already explained everything. I could feel the levels of irritation rising in both her and my husband. I wanted to shout "Wait a minute. I am the patient here. I am the one who may have breast cancer. This is about ME and I do NOT need to be upset by the two of you!" But I said nothing. (In the future I HAD to say/ask for what I needed.)

The surgeon did a quick exam of my breasts. When I asked her opinion, saying I knew she couldn't make a diagnosis at this point but in her experience, what did she think she responded, "Suspicious, highly suspicious."

After leaving her office my husband said, "It is your body, your life, your decision but I wouldn't deal with her. If you can't ask her questions at this point what will it be like going forward?"

At first I thought – I know this surgeon has a good reputation. She is a specialist in this area. Friends who had had breast issues, other than breast cancer, had experienced her as a competent professional. I thought – I won't have to be her patient after the biopsies and possible surgery.

On the other hand after several hours of thinking about my husband's comments I called the surgeon's office and told the receptionist to cancel my scheduled biopsies. I said that I did not think that the doctor and I could have a good working relationship.

I was now on my own. I had no idea what to do next. I didn't want to call the office of the other surgeon whose name I had been given since she was affiliated with the same hospital as the first surgeon. Until this point I had been very calm, but now panic began to set in. How would I find a competent surgeon with whom I could have a good working relationship? (Relationship is very important to me. Good relationships are important to success and I certainly wanted a successful outcome.)

SUGGESTIONS I USED:

- I tried to remember that most lumps/masses/ calcifications are not breast cancer. (I never felt a lump.)
- I don't know why I didn't think of it but I should have called my primary care physician and asked her for recommendations of surgeons when the first one wasn't a good fit for me.
- I took my husband (my support person, later called a "co-patient") with me to my appointments. He has good listening skills (when it comes to other people), is non-emotional, has good, logical thinking and is good at note taking.
- I had friends who would have been honored to have been asked to attend doctors' visits with me.
- In advance of the appointment I wrote down as many questions as I could think of so I could use my time with the doctor efficiently.
- I took a notebook and pencil/pen for both myself and my support person.
- I took notes on what each doctor said. At the top of those notes/answers I wrote the date and the name of the doctor.
- After leaving the appointment I compared notes with those of my support person.
- I began using a 3-ring binder (I started by using folders but found them too cumbersome) in which

to keep important information. I added dividers for the various sections: test results, biopsy reports, radiologist reports, <u>oncologist</u> reports, <u>pathologist</u> reports, bills, insurance reports, etc. as I got further into the process.

- I thought being organized from the beginning would lessen some of the stress later on if this was really a cancer diagnosis. (It is amazing how much I forgot as I got further away from my diagnosis/treatment. At the time this seemed to take over my life.)
- I asked all the questions I needed to ask – sometimes I asked the same question several times.
- I did not feel **very** comfortable with the first surgeon so I found another. I thought I might be dealing with this person for quite awhile so he/she should be someone I liked and trusted.
- In the American Cancer Society booklet "***For Women Facing Breast Cancer***" it is suggested, *"Before having a biopsy you may want to get a second opinion. Using a center that specializes in dealing with breast cancer may be helpful since they will have the most up-to-date research information. The recommendations may be the same but you may find some comfort in knowing that the experts all agree."*
- I asked what training and experience the surgeon had in dealing with breast cancer.
- I asked if there was a patient coordinator (sometimes called a <u>patient navigator</u>) available who might assist me in this unknown new world.

CHAPTER 2

Why Me/Why Not Me????

"What a legacy you have been given – your paternal grandmother and now me with a diagnosis of cancer." Statement to me by my mother - Doris (neither she nor my grandmother had breast cancer) - many years before my diagnosis.

Of course now I started doing an internet search about breast cancer. I wanted to know why I was possibly facing a breast cancer diagnosis since there was no history of breast cancer in our family. (There is a history of other kinds of cancer on both sides of my family.)

There are certain factors that may cause some women to be at greater risk for a breast cancer diagnosis (according to the booklet from the American Cancer Society – *For Women Facing Breast Cancer*) including:

- already had breast cancer;
- been treated with radiation in the chest area;
- close relatives who have had breast or ovarian cancer;
- have BRCA1 and 2 genes (genes that are not working correctly to repair DNA);

- long term use of post-menopausal hormone therapy
- begin menstruating at an early age;
- Menopause at a late age (After menopause, most of a woman's estrogen is made by fat cells. The more fat cells the more estrogen. The majority of breast cancer is estrogen sensitive.);
- no pregnancies;
- first pregnancy after age 30;
- weight gain;
- drinking more than one alcoholic beverage per day;
- not being physically active;
- breasts with dense tissue.

There are some signs to watch for including:

- a lump in the breast;
- changes in consistency or color of breast skin;
- changes in or discharge from the nipple.

I read, in numerous sources, that most breast cancers occur in women with no risk factor other than getting older.

By age **25** 1 in 19,608
By age **30** 1 in 2,525
By age **40** 1 in 217
By age **45** 1 in 93
By age **50** 1 in 50
By age **55** 1 in 33
By age **60** 1 in 24
By age **65** 1 in 17
By age **70** 1 in 14
By age **75** 1 in 11
By age **80** 1 in 10
By age **85** 1 in 9.

The previous statistics were noted in Life Extension Magazine, 2013: p. 48; The Risk of Developing Breast Cancer by Age (from a report by Simone, CB. *Cancer and Nutrition*, Lawrenceville, NJ: Princeton Institute; 2005):

So – Why ME?? I had one of the factors listed that might contribute to a breast cancer diagnosis in addition to getting older. The great sadness of my life was being childless and now I learned this was a factor for breast cancer. As I've known for years – life is not fair.

Age seemed to be the biggest factor. Over the years of cell division, mutations occur. As we age the body loses its ability to repair or destroy these mutated cells.

There was nothing I could do about my age or being childless but there appeared to be a lot I might be able to do to help myself back to health and to a better lifestyle.

CHAPTER 3

Surgeon #2

"If at first you don't succeed - try and try again."
Thomas J. Palmer

Now that I was no longer dealing with the surgeon to whom I had been referred, I didn't know what to do or where to turn. I never thought to call my PCP (Primary Care Physician) who I had known for years and for whom I had a great deal of respect. Looking back, I was much more upset at the time than I thought.

I called several people I knew who worked in the health care field asking them for names of surgeons they had worked with. I asked each person not to say anything to anyone we knew saying I didn't want to upset anyone unnecessarily. Perhaps the mass would turn out to be benign or maybe a cyst. I was finally referred to a Breast Care Center at a hospital in a nearby state.

I read about the facility on-line and called the number that was listed. A real person answered the phone not just a menu of options. (I doubt I could have dealt with computer generated options at that point.) I told the woman how I had been given the news that I had a suspicious mass. I told her about being left standing in the hallway alone for over five minutes before seeing the radiologist and how I decided NEVER to return to that facility. I told her how I planned to write a letter to the head of the facility about my less than compassionate treatment. I explained that I had already seen one surgeon and decided that I could not work with her so I needed to find another. (Did I sound a bit crazed?)

This woman (my patient navigator, though she did not call herself that) was one of the angels that I met on this journey. She helped schedule many of my appointments and dealt with my requests for faxes, etc. over the next couple of months. She always had a smile in her voice and a willingness to listen. I felt as though I had someone on my side that cared.

My "angel" – The Breast Care Coordinator (as she was called at this facility) - made an appointment for me. She requested the reports from the previous surgeon and called to tell me when the reports arrived. She called to "check in" and to ask if there was anything else she could do. She explained that she had been treated for breast cancer. At that time I did not want to hear about her experience but later I was comforted knowing that she knew what I was going through.

My appointment was with a PA (Physician's Assistant), which was fine. I thought that perhaps she would be easier to talk with and would give me more information than a surgeon. Due to a mix-up in scheduling the PA was unavailable so one of the surgeons volunteered to meet with me instead. He said he would stay as long as I needed him to stay to answer my questions. By the time we finished there was no one in the waiting room and the office staff had left for the day. By now I had definitions for all those unknown words the first surgeon had used. I even had definitions for the definitions.

This surgeon was recommending the same procedures as the previous surgeon BUT – he explained exactly what he was recommending and why. He was kind, compassionate, gentle, experienced and had a great sense of humor. (By this point

I needed a few good laughs.) He appeared to be the kind of surgeon I was searching for- one with good clinical skills who was experienced, caring and sensitive. That was my lucky day!!

So began the next phase of this adventure – biopsies.

SUGGESTIONS I USED:

- I wanted to choose my surgeon carefully. I wanted a surgeon who was a mixture of detective, artist and medical advisor who had up-to-date medical research knowledge and excellent communication skills.
- I wanted a surgeon who would give me all the time I needed to ask questions and to make decisions. I knew that he/she would be my expert medical advisor but I also knew **I** wanted to make the decisions I felt were best for me.
- When I didn't understand something I learned to ASK questions. This was a strange new world with a language of its own.
- I took notes and discussed them with my support person after the appointments. I learned quickly to make sure to date and put the doctor's name on the notes I took since I was beginning to drown in paperwork.
- I asked the surgeon how many breast cancer patients he had helped.

CHAPTER 4

Biopsies & the Hypnotist

"Worrying is like a rocking chair; it gives you something to do but doesn't get you anywhere."
Unknown

My surgeon had explained that since I had two different suspicious sites – one a mass and one calcifications, two different biopsies (perhaps called <u>Percutaneous Biopsy</u>) needed to be performed. He said the original mammogram showed a small mass that might be connected to the calcifications and could therefore be much larger. He told me that mammograms only work on a 2-dimensional plane. (<u>3D mammograms</u> are now available though they use twice as much radiation. The difference in terms of the number of cancers found using 3D mammography and conventional mammography is very small says Fran Visco, President of the National Breast Cancer Coalition.)

Dr. Jimenez stated that until the biopsies were completed he could not tell whether there was any malignancy. He said that very often biopsies were negative for cancer but that he wouldn't know until he received the <u>Pathology Report</u>.

I was scheduled for two different biopsies on the same day.

I was told that the type of biopsy is generally determined by the size and location of the suspicious area.

I knew I needed to be calm for the biopsies. One website mentioned <u>hypnosis</u>. I knew that there were drugs I could take to help calm me but I was now focused on having as few chemicals as possible in my body. My body needed to be as healthy as possible to fight this potential cancer.

I did some investigation on the internet, made some calls and found a <u>Hypnotherapist</u> not too far from my home. We spoke for quite awhile on the phone with him answering my many questions. He said he would prefer to see me the morning of the biopsies but since they were scheduled for early on a Monday morning that wasn't possible. He said that seeing him on Friday afternoon would put the percentages for a hypnotic state working at about 75%. That was good enough for me to schedule an appointment.

I had never been to a Hypnotherapist but I thought it couldn't hurt and probably would help. The session was conducted while I sat in a large, comfortable chair. The Hypnotherapist asked me more questions and then told me to close my eyes as he led me through some relaxation exercises. He asked me to tell him in great detail what I thought would be happening to me during the biopsies. At the end of the session I felt very relaxed.

The morning of the biopsies the surgeon's nurse asked if she could accompany me throughout the procedures since she was new to the practice and would like to see how the biopsies were done. Initially I wasn't sure I wanted someone "tagging along" but as I went through the hours of procedures I found it comforting to have her with me; someone to chat with took away some of the angst.

The Outpatient Stereotactic Biopsy (used when the area in question is too small to be felt) uses a special mammography machine to guide the radiologist. I needed to lie on my stomach on a specially designed table where my breast would hang through an opening in the table. The table would be raised and the procedure performed from beneath the table. Computer assisted mammograms would be used to tell where the needle was to be placed for the biopsy. The needle would be used to remove several samples. A small <u>titanium clip/</u> marker was placed in the site so it could be located in the future, if necessary. <u>Local anesthesia</u> was used and no sutures needed.

A guided core biopsy (also called an <u>incisional biopsy</u>) was performed on the "mass" while I was lying on my back. An ultrasound was used to guide the radiologist to the questionable area. Pieces of the mass were removed through the special needle. A titanium clip was placed in the area for future reference, if necessary. Local anesthesia was used and no sutures were needed.

I asked to see the images afterward. I could see the small hooks/clips and was told that these would be removed if surgery was necessary.

Whether it was the hypnosis or not I don't know, but I was able to get through the biopsies with no problems. (After telling the nurse and radiologist how anxious I was the radiologist gave me an A for my calmness.)

SUGGESTIONS I USED:

- I tried to remember that just because I was having a biopsy it did NOT mean that I had cancer.
- I tried to focus on the statement I had read that approximately 80% of biopsies come back negative for cancer.
- I learned that the type of biopsy generally depends upon the size and location of the suspicious area.
- Prior to the biopsies I told the surgeon's nurse about all the medications, vitamins and herbs I was taking. I was told to stop using them in advance of the biopsies

due to the chance of increased bleeding. (I do not take any prescription medications which may have led to different recommendations.)

- On the day of the biopsies I wore a loose shirt that buttoned up the front thinking that this would make it easier afterwards.
- I was concerned about being able to remain still – on my stomach – for 45+minutes. I used the services of a Hypnotherapist but knew there were other methods that could be used to help me be calm.
- I wanted to know what would be happening so asked for a complete explanation (several different times). There were so many words used for these biopsies that I had to keep asking exactly what was going to be done and exactly what the name was for each procedure. This was a nerve-wracking time so I didn't trust myself to hear everything that was being said or to hear it correctly.
- I asked if someone would be needed to drive me home, when could I resume normal activities, if there was anything I should/shouldn't be doing after the biopsies (i.e. exercising, taking supplements/medications, etc.)
- After the biopsies I was good to myself. Even though there was little physical pain involved I knew I had been through an emotionally difficult time. I babied myself. I purchased flowers, read a good book and ate some of my favorite foods the afternoon after the biopsies. If I'd thought of it I would have watched a good movie, too.
- I was told that a <u>Pathologist</u> would examine the specimens and give a written report to the surgeon who would review it with me within the next couple of weeks.
- I made sure I had an appointment scheduled to review the results of the biopsies.
- I made sure my support person could attend the meeting with the Pathologist. I was worried that I would not hear everything or not hear the information correctly.

CHAPTER 5

Pathology Report

"There is so much more right with the body than wrong with it."
Jon Kabat-Zinn

A week after the biopsies I saw Dr. Jimenez to receive the Pathology Report. Again, everyone from the receptionist, to the nurse, to the surgeon was friendly, kind and smiling. (I had made a real effort to learn the names of the receptionists and nurses during my first visit. I knew that these were the people who could be very helpful as I went through this process.) The nurse who had accompanied me through the biopsies greeted me with smiles and a big hug.

Dr. Jimenez reviewed the pathology report with me. Now I had a whole new list of words which, even though Dr. Jimenez defined them for me, I needed to look up when I got home. Of course while he was talking my eyes went immediately to the line **Final Diagnosis**.

The diagnosis was *Ductal Carcinoma, infiltrating*. I was told this meant that I had breast cancer which had moved into the surrounding tissue. This time the size was given in cm (centimeters) which I knew were bigger than millimeters but the smaller number seemed less frightening.

Other words used in the report were: <u>tubule formation</u>, number of <u>mitoses</u>, <u>nuclear pleomorphism</u>, <u>invasion/ invasive/infiltrating</u>, <u>lymphovascular invasion</u>, <u>HER2/NEU</u>, <u>Estrogen</u>, <u>Progesterone</u>, <u>equivocal</u>, <u>FISH Test</u>, <u>ERA</u>, <u>PRA</u>, <u>well-differentiated</u>, <u>stage</u>, <u>proliferation rate</u>, and <u>grade</u>.

The HER2/NEU test results were pending. (I was told that this was a test where positive results were best.)

Out of all those words the ones I heard were "carcinoma" and "invasive"

Dr. Jimenez recommended surgery to remove the tumor. He thought it would probably only (an easy word for him to think and use) require a <u>lumpectomy</u> (not a <u>mastectomy</u>), then <u>radiation</u> and perhaps chemotherapy and then an <u>aromatase inhibitor</u> (an AI - a pill taken daily for a number of years).

I asked how long I could wait before I made a decision as to what to do next. Dr. Jimenez said that this was probably a slow growing cancer so I could take a month or so to decide.

How could he say slow-growing since it had not been seen on the mammogram I had had the year before? When I asked about this I was told that it takes about a million cells for a mass to be detected on a mammogram. I was told that my cancer had probably been growing for about 10 years.

We live within driving distance of one of the medical capitals of the world. I wanted a second opinion from a facility that dealt exclusively with cancer. I was hesitant to make that statement thinking Dr. Jimenez would think I did not trust him. I decided that my life could depend upon the decisions I was about to make. I needed all the information I could possibly obtain to make the best decisions for my care. (This was before reading **For Women Facing Breast Cancer** where they gave this exact advice.)

Dr. Jimenez was not upset by my request. He encouraged me to obtain a second opinion stating that he would like to hear what someone else would recommend. Again, I KNEW I'd made the right decision in using this surgeon/hospital.

I was given a bag of pamphlets from various sources –mostly cancer organizations. I glanced through them and found them to have way too much information. I was so overwhelmed that it was weeks before I read any of them.

I left that appointment saying to my husband, "I do NOT want surgery. I want to see what my other options are." So began my research. I wanted to know if there were ways to shrink the tumor. I was concerned about the possibility that surgery could cause some cells to be left behind and keep growing or start traveling elsewhere. I knew that there was no scientific proof to back up this thought but I had heard it for years and remembered it so, of course, worried about the possibility.

I thought that my life must be out of balance in some way. I needed to look at my spiritual, mental and physical health. I believed I needed to look into the health of my relationships with my family, friends, community and with the air, food and water I was ingesting. I needed to figure out how to live in better harmony with myself and others.

I knew it was imperative to trust all the professionals I would be working with and if someone/something did not "feel right" to me then I needed to find someone/something else.

To win this battle it needed to be a team effort with me being the team leader.

SUGGESTIONS I USED:

- I made sure to take my support person with me to this appointment. I was quite sure that the results would show that I had cancer but I was not sure how I would react to the news. (I am generally quite calm in a crisis but this was a new type of PERSONAL CRISIS.)
- I knew that this appointment would be very important for hearing and understanding what I was being told.

The information I heard would be needed to make the decisions for the next steps.

- I compared notes with my <u>co-patient</u> (what some people call the person going through this experience with the patient) after the appointment.
- I made sure to receive copies of all reports.
- I asked for a definition of every word I did not know. Medical people have their own jargon and forget that many of us have never heard these words before. Different people may use different words to describe the same thing.
- I learned that I should have taken notes on a separate sheet of paper. I realized this when I went to make copies for other professionals and tried to remove the notes I had written on the report. From then on I made a copy of notes, attached it to the report and kept them together in my loose leaf notebook. That way I had a clean copy.
- Though it was difficult, I waited to receive all reports in order to understand my unique situation. This took several weeks, since not all the tests were performed at the same lab.
- I tried not to focus on the results of one test, but to look at all the information as a whole.
- The surgeon told me what he recommended and I asked if there were other options.
- I asked how long I had before I needed to make a decision about what to do next. I did NOT feel rushed to make a decision immediately.
- I found it helpful to give myself an end date for making my decision.
- I wanted a second opinion, so called several of the large cancer centers near my home to see what could be scheduled.

- I learned that a large cancer can be slow-growing and that a small cancer can be fast-growing.
- Though I am not sure it was a good idea I wanted to see what my tumor might look like. We went through a box of raisins until we found one that was close to the measurements I had been given. (Raisins had never looked so big.)
- I learned that the percentage of ER, PR is the number of cells that have receptors out of the 100 cells tested. Having a large number of receptors is helpful if hormonal drugs are recommended.

CHAPTER 6

Second Opinion

A serious illness "is a wakeup call of the highest magnitude."
Patrick Quillin

How would I get a second opinion? Did I have to pay for a second opinion or would medical insurance pay for it? Where would I go to obtain this opinion?

I called a therapist friend and asked her advice about where to obtain a second opinion. She suggested that I call a friend of hers who was dealing with cancer. In the end I called for appointments at a large, well known, highly respected facility that deals exclusively with cancer. The facility is about two hours from our home so could be managed in a day trip.

I was amazed at how easy it was to obtain appointments for a second opinion – one with a surgeon and one with an oncologist. I explained that we would be traveling about two hours and asked if the appointments could be on the same day.

My second opinion surgeon was wonderful, even giving me a hug when I left his office. The oncologist was very efficient. Both told me basically what I had already been told except – I was given the choice of having a mastectomy. The reason given was that, even though it is a more involved operation, I would not need radiation. Since I would no longer have that breast I would not have to worry about a <u>recurrence</u> there. I was told that radiation, if one has already had radiation, is rarely possible if cancer recurs in the same breast. The statistics were now greater for a recurrence- so I would have to face a mastectomy then. Now I had more decisions to make. Should I deal with the "cancer hospital" or the smaller local hospital? Should I choose to have a lumpectomy or a mastectomy? Did I want to deal with either of them or try <u>alternative therapies</u> and have no surgery?

Since I had given myself a month to make up my mind I needed to find out as much as possible as quickly as possible about the options.

SUGGESTIONS I USED:

- I took copies of all the reports I had to the second opinion appointments even though I had been told that the reports had already been sent/faxed.
- I took my notebook and my co-patient to these appointments knowing I would not hear everything that was told to me.
- I paid very close attention to this facility: how easy was it to park; were there other methods of transportation easily available to reach the location; did the cafeteria serve organic foods; how easy was it to navigate the facility; how helpful/friendly was the check-in staff; did the doctors appear rushed/stressed; did the facility offer any complementary medical options; were the doctors willing to do what I requested or did they have set procedures that HAD to be followed; what was the overall "feel" of the facility?
- I asked whether the doctors agreed with the use of Complementary Medical practices. I asked how easily accessible such services would be in terms of cost and

time. I had heard that the cost of complementary and alternative therapies is usually paid for by the patient. I asked if there were any free services available.

- Even though someone I knew "loved" the facility I had to think about myself and what I wanted/needed.
- In the end I decided not to use the facility even though my friend had made the recommendation. I told her that it was not a good fit for me. I didn't tell her that it felt like a huge business where the patients were numbers and research was a very important part of the process. I felt it was too "busy" - too "rushed". The very sick people I saw – with masks and turbans – increased my stress. I tend to be an empathic person so feel the pain/fear as well as the happiness/joy of others.

CHAPTER 7

Telling Friends and Family

"Though no one can go back and make a brand new start,
anyone can start from now and make a brand new ending."
Carl Bard

It's very hard to talk about scary things. Talking about something can make it feel much more real.

I knew that how I told people what was happening to me depended upon who I was telling. I'm not sure how I would have told my husband had I thought about it but he was the first person I saw after receiving the news of a potential breast cancer diagnosis. I probably would have been gentler in my delivery but I just blurted it out. After telling my husband I decided not mention it to any close friends/relatives, thinking I wouldn't worry them until I had a definite diagnosis. Now I had a definite diagnosis.

I learned there was no "right way" to tell people. First, I told my two friends who are dealing with cancer. Then I told another good friend who told her women's group. I realized then that I needed to tell more people since many in her group knew members of my family and mutual friends.

We have three couples that we have socialized with for

years. Telling the three women at one time seemed like a good idea. The bad idea was meeting them for coffee at a local café. One of my friends started to cry and had to run to the ladies' room. I was so engrossed in how I would tell people that I never even thought about how different individuals might react.

I told some friends and family members in person, some by phone, and others by email and skype. In every case I said that the prognosis was very good and not to worry.

SUGGESTIONS I USED:

- I made a list of people I felt **I** needed to tell.
- In telling people I was as positive as possible. I found that, generally, the reaction I received depended upon how I presented the information.
- I asked people to give me a definite amount of time to tell other friends and family before they started telling/talking with others.
- I found that unless people had dealt directly with cancer they found the word very frightening. They knew little about cancer except the worst. (Months later when my 7 year old grandson heard us talking about a friend who had cancer he stated that meant the person was going to die.)
- I told my step-children and sibling (all of whom are adults). I thought it best that they heard what was happening from me. Again, I asked them not to talk about it until I had told all family members. I listened for their response. I shared all the information I had. I let them ask questions. If I didn't have the answers I told them I would get the answers for them.
- Since I had no young children I did not have to deal with this terribly difficult subject with them. Had I had young children I knew to give age appropriate information, encourage questions, make sure they

knew that what was happening was not their fault and to tell school personnel. Children WILL overhear someone else talking about a cancer diagnosis. They will draw their own conclusions which may be far worse than the reality. I do have young step-grandchildren but felt their parents should tell them what was happening if they felt it was appropriate. I knew the grandchildren felt comfortable enough with me that they would ask me questions if they needed to.

- I found it got easier to tell people after I had told the first few.
- I never learned that --- if I needed help I needed to ask. I thought everyone would understand that cards, flowers, offers of meals, visits, calls and rides would mean a lot to me. Many offered/gave but many never did. I still feel badly about that and struggle with questions concerning thoughtfulness and compassion. People don't know what to do but I know a specific offer to help was appreciated (can I drive you to an appointment, what is your favorite food, do you have any allergies, can I drive your children to a practice/game/lesson?) Cards and notes DEFINITELY are appreciated!
- This was a time when I felt very alone. I did not use a support group but in looking back I think it might have been a good idea. I would have learned how other people dealt with their feelings, practical matters, etc.
- We have been involved with the same church for many years. I did call the minister to tell her what was happening but stated that I did not need any help. Again, in looking back, perhaps it would have been better to have said that cards and calls would be welcome. Instead – very few people knew/ acknowledged what was happening.
- I learned that feeling as though I needed to be strong for others might not be the best way to help myself.

CHAPTER 8

In the Meantime

"Learn as if you were going to live forever.
Live as if you were going to die tomorrow."
Mahatma Gandhi

Now that people knew what I was dealing with I started getting advice.

I was suddenly overwhelmed with information. So much of it became just a huge jumble for me. I was driving myself crazy trying to find the "right" sources for me. I found several sources that seemed "right" for me and kept going back to them.

The first piece of advice was in the form of a book that a friend gave me – *Dr. Susan Love's Breast Book* (5th Edition) by Susan M. Love M.D. with Karen Lindsey. The quote from the New York Times, on the cover, reads "The Bible for women with breast cancer".

This book has a wealth of information. The first section is for all women. It tells about the healthy breast and common problems. The rest of the book is for women who have been diagnosed with breast cancer. I am sure it is a good reference book for someone dealing with breast cancer though I found it too overwhelming at the time. I only skimmed it initially. Much later I read the book in sections.

The book explains, in detail, information about the Healthy Breast and Common Problems. It then discusses what causes breast cancer and how to prevent it, diagnosis and screening (including biopsies, how to read reports), surgeries, treatment options, lifestyle changes, Complementary treatments, decisions, treatments, recurrence, drugs, websites, and a Pathology Checklist.

I was given another book *"The Answer to Cancer Is Never Giving it a_Chance to Start"* by Sharma, Mishra and Meade. This book contains <u>Ayurveda</u> knowledge presented in an interesting and humorous way. (I needed more humor by now.) The authors state that cancer is a "sickness from the deepest level of your body –a mix-up in the <u>DNA</u>". There are suggestions for diet, meditation, exercise, sleep, <u>detox</u>, breathing exercises, yoga exercises and how not to get sick from chemo.

I had read somewhere that Suzanne Somers was a breast cancer survivor and had written a book about it. A little online research and a trip to the local bookstore brought me to her book entitled *Knockout*.

Knockout contains a list of resources, the names of Complementary and <u>Naturopathic</u> doctors (listed by state) and information about the Life Extension Foundation. This book is about cancer – not just breast cancer. I found it to be very helpful. It gave me ideas of what to do next.

The Life Extension Foundation is a non-profit organization working to find new ways of dealing with many diseases, including cancer (www.lef.org). There is a phone number you can call to speak with a doctor. If you call with a question a doctor will return your call. I spoke with several different doctors over the next several weeks. All were very helpful and gave me as much time as I needed. There are many helpful downloadable articles available on their website.

SUGGESTIONS I USED:

- I needed to remember to "Think for myself." This was not easy to do since I knew so little about cancer and what options there might be for treating it.
- I often listened to the advice of others then needed time to decide what was best for me.
- I learned, early on, to be very careful about what sources I used. I needed to know who was writing the source I was reading. I needed to pay attention to what was being recommended/reported in reference to the kind of breast cancer **I** had.
- I learned that chat rooms/blogs often only gave one point of view. I realized that people who are not having a problem with drugs/therapies may not be using these websites/chatrooms so the thoughts expressed may be one-sided.

CHAPTER 9

The Herbalist

"Your problem just became your stepping stone.
Catch the moment."
This was the saying inside my fortune
cookie just after diagnosis.

I called my friend who had been seeing an herbalist for his prostate cancer. Again, I thought, "I have nothing to lose, why not make an appointment." My most important question was, "Are there other less invasive ways to remove a cancerous tumor than by having surgery?"

The Herbalist had years of experience. He told me about Essiac Tea. This tea is a mixture of several herbs, including sheep sorrel, burdock root, slippery elm, turkey rhubarb root and red clover. It was first made by Renee Caisse, R.N. (Essiac is her last name spelled backwards) who was treating cancer patients in Canada in the 1920's. The idea is that this tea will stimulate the body's own self-healing capabilities. I initially purchased dried herbs and made my own Essiac tea. Though less expensive than buying it already prepared, I found making my own to be stressful. (I purchased the herb mixture from Jean's Greens www.jeansgreens.com. I have also seen it advertised through ESSIAC Canada International though with a little different selection of herbs.) After the first try I decided that buying it already made was what I needed to do.

This was the first time I had heard that "Cancer loves sugar; it feeds on sugar." This fact seemed so important. I was shocked that I had never heard this before. Though it is nearly impossible not to eat sugar I wanted to decrease the amount of refined sugar I was ingesting. This meant trying to avoid sugar of any color, beet or cane – as well as high fructose corn syrup.

I learned that sugar suppresses the immune system.

I was told that carbohydrates and sucrose are converted to glucose (blood sugar) which is the primary source of energy for the body. Insulin is needed to process the glucose. Too much glucose means the body has to work harder to process it. Most things we eat are ultimately turned to glucose by our body.

I was told that cancer likes an acidic body. (See Chapter 11) I read that Epsom Salt baths might help to eliminate toxins and raise the pH (potential of Hydrogen – see Chapter 11) level. I filled the tub with hot water - as hot as I could tolerate. I then stirred in 3 cups of Epsom Salt, 16 oz. of hydrogen peroxide and a small amount of baking soda. I tried to sit in the tub for approximately 15-20 minutes. (I was told by the radiation people not to submerge my breast in hot tub water while undergoing radiation therapy and not to expose it to the direct sunlight. At that point I found a way to soak in my bath but keeping my one breast out of the water. Awkward but, I felt, relaxing.) I found my tub to be too shallow to allow me to submerge most of my body so I used duct tape to cover the water outlet. I watched this carefully since I did not need the added problem of flooding my bathroom because of the blocked overflow outlet. I also purchased a bath ball (www.cuzn.com) filter to go over the faucet to filter out the chlorine in the town water. (The steamy water of a hot bath opens your pores and allows the body to soak up chlorine. Chlorine is a powerful chemical. Water is chlorinated to kill bacteria but the chlorine, reportedly, can damage our skin, hair, etc.)

Fluoride and chlorine are both considered, by some experts (www.mercola.com); to be carcinogenic. I called our town water department to find out if chlorine was added to our town water. I was told that it was added but there are easy ways to reduce it – use a whole house filter (which can be very expensive), individual carbon filters (a Brita filtered water pitcher and the Camelbak filtered water bottle both worked well – and continue to work well – for me) or just fill a container with tap water and let it sit for a couple of hours. Fluoride is often added to a town/city water supply in an effort to reduce cavities. According to Fluoride Action Network (Boston Globe, February 1, 2015) "excessive fluoride exposure has been linked to many ailments, including arthritis, glucose intolerance, gastrointestinal distress, thyroid disease, and possibly cardiovascular disease and some cancers". I was served some reverse osmosis water at a health foods restaurant and couldn't believe how wonderful it tasted – so different from the water I was used to drinking – but this was a special treat not something I was able to use on a regular basis.

Another piece of information the Herbalist gave me was that cancer likes a body that is oxygen poor (anaerobic). To get more oxygen into my body I tried deep breathing and exercising to increase the depth and amount of oxygen I was getting. One technique I tried, that took little effort, was to lie on the floor and place a book on my abdomen. As I inhaled I tried to make my abdomen expand and the book rise. Though, I think, it is better to exercise hard enough to break a sweat, I used this exercise on days when my energy level was low. I tried to exercise at least 30 minutes daily but I could only do what I could do; many days this did not happen. Exercising also assists the Lymphatic System (See Chapter 13) in moving and eliminating toxins. My doctor did a simple test to determine my oxygen levels by placing a small clamplike device on my finger.

The suggestion was made that I try deep tissue massages. Massages are reported to release toxins, increase blood circulation and decrease inflammation. I thought that massages couldn't hurt and would feel wonderfully relaxing. (I have heard that some doctors discourage such massages so make sure to check this with your medical provider.)

The Herbalist talked about vitamins. I had been taking a daily vitamin for years but he was talking specifically about Vitamin D3. More and more research is being done on the body's need for Vitamin D3. There are some who say that cancer likes a body that is low in Vitamin D3. To raise my vitamin D3 levels I tried to be outdoors in the sunlight with as much skin exposed as possible, using no sunblock, for about 15 minutes around noontime. Many medical experts say that this short time will not cause an increase in skin cancer but will increase Vitamin D3 levels. I learned that if one lives in the Northeast or any high latitude region raising Vitamin D3 levels this way is almost impossible from mid-October through mid-March. I began taking vitamin D3 supplements. The recommended amount for people dealing with cancer is higher than the RDA (recommended daily amount) listed by the government. A Harvard Medical School Study suggests that everyone with cancer should take 5,000 IU's a day (www. canceractive.com).

Homes built on underground water or too close to high tension wires are thought, by some, to put additional stress on the body. Cell phones may stress the body. (There is conflicting research on these issues.) Whether I believed this or not it seemed to make sense to move the phone, clock radio, etc. away from the headboard of the bed where I slept and to try to decrease the amount of exposure.

The Herbalist told me all of the above would contribute to my better health but that I would have to make the decision

about surgery for myself. He told me what I already knew --
People could give me advice but in the end all decisions were
mine to make.

SUGGESTIONS I USED:

- I drank Essaic Tea even though I had heard that there
  was no scientific support of it being helpful. I thought
  that something made of common weeds couldn't be
  harmful – and might help. Plus drinking tea seemed
  relaxing.
- Since many sources reported that cancer likes sugar
  I began to decrease the amount of refined sugar I
  ingested.
- I began reading the label on every food product I
  purchased to determine the amount of sugar that it
  contained.
- I tried to get and keep my body as close as possible
  to pH neutral since I had read in many sources that
  cancer likes an acidic body.
- I read that cancer likes a body that is oxygen poor so I
  attempted to increase the amount of oxygen in my body
  by exercising and using deep breathing techniques.
- I had read that cancer likes a body with less than
  average body temperature so I tried to raise my body
  temperature, by exercising, until I was perspiring.
  Though I doubt this was helpful – again it couldn't hurt.
- I insisted that my Vitamin D3 levels be tested since I
  had read that high Vitamin D3 levels were good in the
  war against cancer.
- I began drinking filtered water as often as possible.
- I tried coffee enemas, having heard that they might be
  helpful. This was not something I tried more than a
  couple of times even though I had read a number of
  positive comments.

CHAPTER 10

The Naturopath

"Your mission is to make your body so full of wellness that
there is no room for illness."
Patrick Quillin

I had met a child who had bitten his teacher on the first day
of kindergarten. His mother removed him from school and
worked with a Naturopath. Five months later he returned to
school a different child. The Naturopath had determined that
he had multiple food sensitivities and worked with him and
his family. I thought that if it worked for him perhaps I might
learn something helpful from a Naturopathic Doctor.

A Naturopath believes in the body's ability to heal itself
by creating a healthy environment both inside and outside.
Naturopathic Doctors combine the wisdom of nature with
modern science.

Naturopathic Medicine is sometimes called Naturopathy
or Natural Medicine. It is a form of alternative medicine
which uses many natural treatments including: herbs,
massage, exposure to the natural elements, nutrition
advice, supplements, hydrotherapy, clinical and lab tests,
acupuncture and teaching stress management techniques.

The doctor educates the patient in ways which might help physically, mentally, emotionally, environmentally, socially and/or spiritually.

Naturopaths are licensed in some states as a ND or NMD but many states have no requirements. Their education varies widely.

Naturopaths are often criticized for the use of unproven, controversial therapies. The US National Center for Complementary and Alternative Medicine has published the following, "Naturopathy as a general approach to health care has not been widely researched".

I thought a Naturopath might be helpful to me at this point. I remembered the name of the Naturopath who worked with the above mentioned child and found her in a nearby town.

Though my insurance did not pay for her services, I felt it was something I needed to explore. Our first meeting consisted of a lengthy interview about my past medical history and my current diagnosis. She told me of her fight with breast cancer. It was helpful to know that she had personal experience with this disease.

SUGGESTIONS I USED:

- The American Association of Naturopathic Physicians can be quite helpful in locating a doctor.
- I did not use but have since learned that there is a specialist in the field called a <u>Naturopathic Oncologist</u>. Had I known that at the time I would have attempted to find one in my area.

CHAPTER 11

pH balancing

"One of the best ways to survive cancer is to fight back."
Bernie Siegel

I knew nothing about pH other than what I remembered from high school chemistry about changing the color of litmus paper. The Herbalist had made a point of telling me that my pH needed to be as balanced as possible so now I needed to know more.

Various sources stated that cancer thrives in an acidic environment. The opposite of acidic is <u>alkaline</u>.

pH stands for "potential of Hydrogen". Any slight decrease in the pH levels in the blood will result in lower oxygen levels in the blood and cells. Some say that cancer HATES an oxygen rich environment and a more alkaline environment is better to have. I tried for a balance between an acidic body and an alkaline one. I had heard that a highly acidic body causes decreased energy while an alkaline one can help with increased energy. Whether that was true or not I thought why not try becoming more alkaline. It couldn't hurt.

pH levels can be tested using test strips purchased at a drugstore or online. They are used to test saliva or urine.

Directions for testing are given on/in the box with color charts to match the color of the strip after it has been placed in the saliva/urine. I tested my saliva first thing in the morning (or I could have tested it two hours after eating) by spitting into a spoon, dipping the strip and comparing the color to that on the chart. Sometimes I tested my urine first thing in the morning by filling a small cup with urine, dipping the test strip in and then comparing it to the color chart. This is a general indicator of the acidity level at the particular time when tested. I knew this was testing the pH in a fluid not what was stored in my body tissues/blood but I thought it was helpful in watching what I ate.

There are scientists who believe that cancer is caused by a virus. Whether this is true or not remains to be proven. Viruses (fungi and bacteria, too) thrive and survive in an acidic environment. This was another reason to try to have my body become more alkaline.

Diet is the most important change I could make to balance my natural pH -and I didn't even know if changing my diet would help but it couldn't hurt. Processed and refined foods are said to be extremely acidic to our systems. I avoided overconsumption of meat, alcohol, soft drinks, caffeine, eggs, vinegar, cheese, coffee, sugar, white flour and artificial sweeteners.

Different experts seem to have different ideas on how to make the body more alkaline using the diet. Most suggest the following: adding raw vegetables such as kale, broccoli, cabbage, cauliflower, brussels sprouts, tomatoes (they become alkaline in the body even though they taste acidic) to the diet; adding fruits but in limited amounts with the following being the most recommended: apples (with the skins), cherries, lemons (though they taste acidic they become alkaline in the body), mangos, oranges, peaches, pears and pineapple. Vegetables are recommended more than fruit because of the high sugar content of many fruits (though that is offset a bit by the fiber content).

The chart below was taken from the online Natural Health School www.naturalhealthschool.com

pH Balance Chart

Most Alkaline	Alkaline	Lowest Alkaline	FOOD CATEGORY	Lowest Acid	Acid	Most Acid
Stevia	Maple Syrup, Rice Syrup	Raw Honey, Raw Sugar	SWEETENERS	Processed Honey, Molasses	White Sugar, Brown Sugar	NutraSweet, Equal, Aspartame, Sweet 'N Low
Lemons, Watermelon, Limes, Grapefruit, Mangoes, Papayas	Dates, Figs, Melons, Grapes, Papaya, Kiwi, Blueberries, Apples, Pears, Raisins	Oranges, Bananas, Cherries, Pineapple, Peaches, Avocados	FRUITS	Plums, Processed Fruit Juices	Sour Cherries, Rhubarb	Blackberries, Cranberries, Prunes
Asparagus, Onions, Vegetable Juices, Parsley, Raw Spinach, Broccoli, Garlic	Okra, Squash, Green Beans, Beets, Celery, Lettuce, Zucchini, Sweet Potato, Carob	Carrots, Tomatoes, Fresh Corn, Mushrooms, Cabbage, Peas, Potato Skins, Olives, Soybeans, Tofu	BEANS VEGETABLES LEGUMES	Cooked Spinach, Kidney Beans, String Beans	Potatoes (without skins), Pinto Beans, Navy Beans, Lima Beans	Chocolate
	Almonds	Chestnuts	NUTS SEEDS	Pumpkin Seeds, Sunflower Seeds	Pecans, Cashews	Peanuts, Walnuts
Olive Oil	Flax Seed Oil	Canola Oil	OILS	Corn Oil		
		Amaranth, Millet, Wild Rice, Quinoa	GRAINS CEREALS	Sprouted Wheat Bread, Spelt, Brown Rice	White Rice, Corn, Buckwheat, Oats, Rye	Wheat, White Flour, Pastries, Pasta
			MEATS	Venison, Cold Water Fish	Turkey, Chicken, Lamb	Beef, Pork, Shellfish
	Breast Milk	Soy Cheese, Soy Milk, Goat Milk, Goat Cheese, Whey	EGGS DAIRY	Eggs, Butter, Yogurt, Buttermilk, Cottage Cheese	Raw Milk	Cheese, Homogenized Milk, Ice Cream
Herb Teas, Lemon Water	Green Tea	Ginger Tea	BEVERAGES	Tea	Coffee	Beer, Soft Drinks

Note that a food's acid or alkaline-forming tendency in the body has nothing to do with the actual pH of the food itself. For example, lemons are very acidic, however the end-products they produce after digestion and assimilation are very alkaline so lemons are alkaline-forming in the body. Likewise, meat will test alkaline before digestion but it leaves acidic residue in the body so meat is acid-forming.

pH Balance Chart

For proper digestion HCL (hydrochloric acid) levels need to be good. Probiotics may help with this.

Dr. Theodore Baroody in his book *Alkalize or Die* (see bibliography) lists foods to eat and those to avoid. He also suggests meals for three weeks to help with alkalizing your system.

SUGGESTIONS I USED:

- I tried to increase my HCL levels by using the suggestion in Dr. Baroody's book (see bibliography) of 2 tablespoons of apple cider vinegar and 1 tsp of honey in water before each meal. Though vinegar is said to increase acidity I thought raising my HCL levels to improve digestion was most important.

- I began to chew my food more. I knew that the saliva in my mouth starts the digestion process so thought that the more I chewed the less my stomach would have to work to digest food.
- I read in several places that the vegetables/herbs that are recommended to be helpful are: mushrooms, onions, parsley, parsnips, bell peppers, sweet potatoes, spinach, squash, peas, string beans, almonds and sprouted seeds. It was suggested that if I had to eat white potatoes to eat the skins, too,
- I learned that the foods to avoid were: breads, crackers, pastries, shrimp, lobster, bacon, milk and milk products (the sharper the cheese the more acid producing it is – I began using goat cheese and plain Greek yogurt), meat, eggs, all processed foods, wheat, corn, soy (though there is controversy about this), corn meal (most corn and soy is <u>genetically modified</u>) and white rice.
- Since it seemed as though there was nothing left to eat that I liked I tried using Dr. Baroody's suggestion of eating eight out of ten items that are alkalizing.
- I began using stainless steel pots, pans and cooking utensils.
- I learned that what I put ON my skin (my largest organ) is absorbed and therefore taken into my body. I began using organic body washes/creams/cosmetics.
- I tried to eat more foods high in <u>omega 3's</u> ("good fat" found in fish, some nuts, and some vegetables). Omega 3's help with cell functioning.
- I tried to avoid overconsumption of <u>omega 6's</u> (sunflower oil, corn oil, safflower oil, salad dressing and mayonnaise, snacks, fast foods, cookies, etc.) which can cause inflammation to worsen. There needs to be a good balance between omega 3's and omega 6 – which is difficult to obtain with our modern western diet.
- I tried using a probiotic to help with digestion.

CHAPTER 12

The Immune System

"Tumor cells turn off the immune system, preventing it from attacking."
Dr. Philip A. Sharp (MIT researcher quoted
in Parade Magazine August 31, 2014)

The <u>Immune System</u> protects the body against disease. I knew my immune system must be compromised since it had not killed off the cancer cells that had grown to the mass I was now dealing with. (I had heard that most people have cancer cells in their bodies but the cells are killed by the immune system before becoming a problem.)

After surgery my immune system would be weakened - a welcome hostess for bacteria, fungi, viruses, etc. I had several weeks to work on strengthening my immune system, not a long time but what I had.

Though I was told that there is no scientifically proven link between a better immune system and one's lifestyle, I thought there had to be. I HAD to make my immune system as strong as possible in order to deal, in the best way possible, with what was ahead. I certainly did not want to be dealing with some other disease (even the miserable common cold) while my body was recovering and trying to fight off any cancer cells that might not have been removed.

The immune system is a very complex system made up of the skin, nose, eyes, mouth, thymus, spleen, lymph (see Chapter 13), bone marrow, white blood cells, antibodies, hormones and many other unknowns.

I started trying to build up as many of the parts of my immune system as possible.

I was told that cancer loves an anaerobic (oxygen poor) body. I knew that I needed to be getting more oxygen to my cells. I started to exercise more – though there were days when I could do no more than bounce on my mini-trampoline for a few minutes or walk in front of the TV. Did this help? I don't know but it did make me feel better.

On the weekends we would go to our cabin in Vermont where the air seemed cleaner and the water, directly from our mountain spring, seemed more refreshing. I felt better, stronger just being in nature. I thought that since trees give off oxygen there might be more oxygen in the forest than in the city. It may have all been in my head – but a lot of the fight against cancer had to be in my head. I had to have the right attitude and if part of that was believing something was helping then perhaps it was.

I also had heard that cancer does not like heat. I thought that if I could break a sweat by exercising it might mean that my body temperature was up. I knew I couldn't get my temperature as high as the scientists do in the lab to kill cancer cells, but perhaps a little exercising would raise my body temperature and be helpful to my mind and spirit.

The baths mentioned in chapter 8 became an almost nightly ritual. I found these to be very relaxing at the end of the day. Also, because they made me perspire a lot, I thought they might be helpful in raising my body temperature and removing toxins.

There have always been two things I was good at - sleeping

and eating. Now I was not sleeping well. I knew that quality of sleep was imperative to having a strong immune system. During sleep the body repairs itself. During sleep my body needed to renew itself for the fight ahead, for another day. I tried a number of different ways to improve the quality of my sleep, though never used prescription sleep aids.

I started taking various supplements as described in Chapter 15, and began paying more attention to the foods I ate, what was in them, where they came from, and how they were prepared.

My liver became a focal point. I knew that the liver is an important organ for filtering toxins from the blood. The liver neutralizes toxins and then moves them to the small intestine which moves them to the large intestine and then out of the body. If the liver doesn't do its job properly then the toxins are reabsorbed into the blood. I read that all of the blood in the body passes through the liver quite rapidly. I wanted those toxins (including dead cancer cells) out of my body as quickly as possible.

I found the following information from *Mother Earth News* (August/September 2014) to be concise and helpful:

> Things that weaken the immune system: chronic infections, stress overload, obesity, aging, insufficient sleep, depression, anxiety.
>
> Things that strengthen the immune system: probiotics, healing herbs, moderate exercise, ample sleep, meditation, laughter.

SUGGESTIONS I USED:

Remember to consult your health care provider before making any changes to your diet or using any supplements or herbs.

- To strengthen my immune system I needed adequate amounts of protein, vitamins and minerals. Herbs like Echinacea (some people with allergies to ragweed have an adverse reaction), Astragalus and mushroom extracts were suggested. I continue to use both Echinacea and Astragalus especially in the winter in New England.
- I needed to reduce stress.
- I needed to decrease my intake of carbohydrates.
- I needed to reduce eating excessively fatty meals.
- I needed to get enough good quality sleep.
- I needed to deal with feelings of depression.
- I needed to eliminate as many toxins, from my body, as possible.
- I started taking the supplement melatonin to try to get a better night's sleep. Initially I didn't read the label well so did not realize that I should discontinue taking it for a week every couple of months. I started by taking a low dose.
- I began taking the supplement magnesium since I had heard that older adults have decreased amounts and it can help with improving sleep. I needed to adjust the amounts since initially this caused diarrhea.
- To improve my sleep I stopped using any screens (i.e. TV, computer, eBook, etc.) within an hour of bedtime.
- I tried to have a regular sleep schedule and to eat a small amount of protein (I tried one tablespoon of almond butter) before going to bed.
- I requested that my vitamin D3 levels be tested. The amount of vitamin D3 decreases in the body as we age. There is a great deal written about the need for higher Vitamin D3 levels than those that have been recommended in the past.
- I tried being outside in the sunlight with as much skin exposed as possible (without sunscreen) for 15 minutes

a day – which is said to help the body make vitamin D3 during summer time only at higher latitudes.

- I began using fish oil in larger amounts than the RDA (recommended daily amount by the Federal Drug Administration). I always checked the Omega 3 amounts per serving and also the amount of EPA and DHA. Of great importance is quality.
- I began exercising on a regular basis.
- I began doing a walking exercise program found on On Demand TV. There are various types of good exercise programs there–easy to very strenuous. There are also many cds, videos and fitness club programs available.
- I began using an eye mask in order to make my bedroom as dark as possible.
- I moved our clock radio and phone away from the head of the bed.
- I turned on our electric blanket to warm our bed and then turned it off before getting into bed for the night.
- I stopped drinking all soft drinks especially those containing aspartame. (Dr. Richard Wurtman of MIT has done extensive research on aspartame. He states that aspartame is neurologically toxic and increases the appetite.)
- I had been using soy milk for a number of years. I now began using almond milk. Most soy is reported to be genetically modified. Soy has been shown to be a powerful aromatase stimulator. I had an estrogen positive tumor so it made sense to me not to consume soy even though the estrogen is different. There is a great deal of controversy around this issue.
- I began using Iscador. Iscador is derived from the mistletoe plant; it has been used for centuries in some European countries for the remission of cancer. It is approved and paid for by the German government for

use with cancer patients. It is also used to build up the Immune System. It is NOT approved by the USDA.

- I wanted to get my temperature up. I used exercise and hot baths even though there is no research to support these methods.
- To calm and relax my mind I started using the cd's from the *Mindfulness Based Stress Reduction Program*. This is a program which is offered through the University of Massachusetts Medical Center during weekly sessions. Since I had neither the time nor the money to enroll in the program I decided I'd try the cd's offered. This program incorporates breathing, yoga, and meditation. (See the reference section for more information).
- I tried to be outside as much as possible especially in the woods.
- I started putting a quarter sized portion of iodine on my thigh every day since I had read that Iodine increases cancer protection. I had been told that if the iodine was absorbed rapidly my body needed more iodine.
- I started being able to say there were things I couldn't do, didn't want to do. I was finding my voice and was able to say no to things that I did not find enjoyable.
- I tried to remember the saying I heard about relationships – Cultivate the ones that feed you don't bleed you.
- I had learned that cancer LOVES sugar. I stopped eating additional sugars as much as possible.
- I began paying more attention to the foods I ate, especially watching the level of carbohydrates and sugars. Label reading became a big part of food buying and preparation.
- I tried castor oil wraps with heat for liver cleansing. Directions come in the wool flannel package that can

be purchased at the drug store. This was messy but did give me a chance to relax during the day.

- I found an <u>Integrative Medicine Doctor</u> in our area. She was able to guide me in strengthening my immune system before surgery, before starting radiation treatments.
- I found a Naturopathic Physician who was helpful in suggesting supplements and other life changes.
- I made a point of washing my hands often.
- I attempted to stay away from people who were sick.
- I stopped shaking hands.
- I used an antibacterial hand cleaner when out in public.

CHAPTER 13

The Lymphatic System

(A Part of the Immune System)

"Never, never give up!" Winston Churchill

Years ago a friend who had breast cancer struggled with lymphedema that was caused by the removal of lymph nodes during her breast cancer operation. This was something I did NOT want to deal with.

I knew very little about the Lymphatic System. I had been told that the surgeon would be removing at least one sentinel node when he removed the tumor IF I agreed to lymph node removal. I knew that sentinel nodes are part of the Lymphatic System.

The Lymphatic System plays an important part in the Immune System - which protects the body against disease. The Lymphatic System is comprised of tiny vessels with one way valves which carry a protein rich clear/whitish fluid containing white blood cells (lymphocytes- NK – natural killer cells) to all parts of the body. It also picks up waste material, such as dead cells and toxins, and moves it upward toward the heart/neck where it enters the bloodstream. The waste material is returned to the blood vessels for removal through the kidneys, liver, lungs, skin, etc. The upper right quadrant, right arm, right side of the head and neck drain on the right side of the neck while the rest of the body drains on the left side of the neck (from internet article written by The Editors of Encyclopedia Britannica updated 9-8-2014)

The Lymphatic System has no pump to move the fluid through the body, as the heart does for the blood. The system works through the movement of the muscles of the body.

There are 600-700 Lymph Nodes, found in clusters in the average body. These are part of the Lymphatic System. Most are in the neck, armpit, groin, center of the chest and in the abdomen. The largest number is clustered around the intestinal tract. They sit on the intestinal wall and keep dangerous bacteria in the gut from migrating into the blood stream. The nodes produce immune cells that help the body fight infection. Nodes swell when there is an overproduction of infection fighting white blood cells. Common areas where they can be felt are the groin, armpit, behind the ears, back of the head, side of the neck and under the jaw and chin.

These nodes filter the lymph before it passes into the circulatory system. Lymph nodes can trap cancerous cells. If a node gets "overrun" with cancer cells then the cells can be carried to other parts of the body (metastases). Nodes do not regenerate.

It would seem to make sense for everyone – whether one is dealing with cancer or would just like to avoid colds and flu - to strengthen the Immune System, to move toxins out of the body quickly. One helpful way to do this is by skin brushing. This can be done with a brush purchased at the drugstore or health foods store or by using an air dried towel (much rougher than those dried in the dryer). There are YouTube videos and detox books explaining the process but basically it is brushing the skin starting at the feet and brushing toward the heart for 5-15 minutes per day in the morning before your shower.

Prior to my breast cancer surgery radioactive material would be injected into the breast. It would "light up" those nodes (sentinel node/s) closest to the tumor site. These would be the first nodes that any of the cancer cells would go to if they had moved from the tumor. These are the nodes that are removed for testing. Generally lymph nodes in the armpit (<u>axillary lymph nodes</u>) are the first to be removed and examined to see if they contain cancer cells.

After learning these facts I decided that I needed to give permission for my sentinel node/s to be removed. Dr. Jimenez stated that this would give another piece of necessary information to help me make future decisions. Whether the nodes contained cancer cells or not was information I needed.

<u>SUGGESTIONS I USED</u>:

- I asked about the possibility of lymphedema and what could be done to avoid it if any lymph nodes were removed.
- I learned that exercise can help speed the process of moving the lymphatic fluid through the body. As a good, gentle exercise to help with this I started walking and purposely gently swinging my arms.
- I bought a rebounder (Mini Rounder – mini trampoline - for about $50.) which I used both before and after my surgery. It was awhile after surgery before I could tolerate the bouncing of my breast even using a sports' bra.
- I used skin brushing before my bath/shower to help move the lymph.
- I knew that massage was helpful for stress and painful muscles. I read that massage was also good for helping move the lymphatic fluid. I had my massage therapist give me several lymphatic massages after my surgery. I should have cleared having this type (or any type)

of massage with my surgeon beforehand but never thought of it until a friend told me that her surgeon said not to have massages.

- I gave myself gentle rhythmic massages on the arm on the operated side using long, light strokes.
- Though it has never been proven to help I decided that it made sense to stop wearing a bra. I thought that if gentle massage helps the lymph system then having breasts hang free would be a natural massage.
- I decided to begin wearing natural (unbleached) organic cotton clothing next to my skin. I purchased an unbleached, organic cotton camisole. I thought it was expensive but worth the money.
- I used organic unscented deodorant and body lotion as well as organic shampoo, conditioner, toothpaste and facial cleanser. It made sense to me to keep as many toxins off my skin as possible since all of these products are readily absorbed through the skin.
- I decided to allow the removal of the sentinel node/s since that seemed to be a way to determine if the cancer might have spread. I needed that information in order to make the next decisions.
- I had read that drinking water would help my lymphatic system function better so I began trying to drink at least six 8 ounce glasses of filtered water a day.

CHAPTER 14

Eating for Better Health

"Let food be thy medicine and medicine be thy food."
Hippocrates - Ancient Greek Physician

I needed to start eating better to give my body the best possible chance for recovery and then long term health. There are so many articles, magazines, books on what to eat, how to eat, when to eat. I needed to find what would work best for ME.

I had read about superfoods including: garlic (considered, by many, to be an exceptional food), broccoli, brussels sprouts, cabbage, kale, cauliflower, mushrooms, legumes (beans, lentils, etc.) apples, berries (tend to be lower in fructose – fruit sugar – than other fruits), citrus fruits, ginger and spinach among many others. I had just so much time and energy so found a few recipes that were easy and that I liked and then used supplements.

Other highly nutritious foods include: fermented foods (kefir, pickles, sauerkraut, olives), free range eggs, grass fed beef, unpasteurized (raw) milk from grass-fed cows, coconut oil, krill oil and matcha green tea made with filtered water.

Foods that have high alkalinity (I was striving for balanced pH levels) in the body are: tomatoes, limes, avocados, white navy beans, beets, radishes, cucumbers, kale, apricots, mangoes, goat's milk and goat cheese, flaxseed oil, olive oil, wild rice, quinoa, almonds, *raw* spinach, green beans, sweet potatoes, squash, zucchini, onions, lemons, blueberries, stevia (instead of sugar), celery, carrots, romaine lettuce and dried figs.

Some of the foods which produce acid in the body (which I wanted to avoid) are: meat, seafood, eggs, cow's milk, sweet fruits, cheese made from cow's milk, grains, junk food, peanuts, walnuts, cashews, lima beans, pinto beans, kidney beans, cranberries, blackberries, prunes and yogurt.

I learned that a glass of fruit juice is often loaded with fructose. Most of the antioxidants have been lost in the processing. It is far better to eat the whole fruit since there are vitamins and other antioxidants which will offset some of the effects of a rapid rise in blood sugar levels. (Fructose is absorbed immediately, going straight to your liver.) 25-30 grams of fructose per day is the recommended maximum. If I wanted to drink a glass of fruit juice (or wine) I would drink it on a full stomach so it would be absorbed more slowly causing less stress to the liver.

The Environmental Working Group (EWG is a non-profit group focused on public health) has reviewed nearly 100,000 produce pesticide reports from the USDA and USFA. They are attempting to determine which fruits and vegetables have the highest amounts of chemical residue. Fruits and vegetables with soft skins tend to absorb more pesticides. Those with a strong outer layer are less toxic since the outer layer provides a defense against pesticide absorption. The EWG (Environmental Working Group www.ewg.org) website is very informative.

Buying organic can be quite expensive. There are numerous listings of The Dirty Dozen Plus. These are the items to buy organic. This list seems to change periodically but at the present time (2016) it is suggested that one buy the following organically grown, if at all possible: apples, peaches, celery, strawberries, spinach, nectarines, grapes, cherries, sweet bell peppers, cherry tomatoes, lettuce, cucumbers and tomatoes plus hot peppers and Kale/Collard Greens. (Environmental Working Group).

There is also a list of The Clean 15. These are fruits and vegetables that you do not need to buy organically. This list, too, changes from time to time: onions, sweet corn, pineapples, avocados, asparagus, sweet peas (frozen), mangoes, eggplant, honeydew melon, kiwi, cabbages, grapefruit, cauliflower, cantaloupe and papayas. (www.drweil.com)

If I couldn't find or couldn't afford to buy The Clean 15 I removed the pesticides from a fruit/vegetable by soaking it for about 5 minutes in a gallon of lukewarm water with 2 tablespoons of vinegar added. Then I would rinse and brush with a vegetable brush. Another possibility is to soak the fruits and/or vegetables in a solution of 4 tablespoons of salt and the juice of ½ of a fresh lemon added to a sinkful of water for about 10 minutes. I, also, tried to wash everything with a natural fruit/veggie wash that I purchased at the store. When I couldn't find organically grown fruits and vegetables that were supposed to be good for me I decided that eating the nonorganic ones probably outweighed not eating them at all.

I wanted to eat food that are easy to digest – taking as much stress off my digestive system as possible. To make vegetables easier to digest I tried steaming them, using filtered water, for a few minutes to break down some of the plant cells.

I stopped eating farm raised fish (even if it was salmon which is supposed to be so good for me). I read that farm raised fish are, generally, kept in "pens", fed soy and antibiotics with some even being fed a dye to improve the color. I started eating fish labeled "wild caught". I also tried to only buy fish that were caught in U.S. or Canadian waters.

Cancer is said to be highly dependent on iron for nutrition. (www.pcrm.org>health>nutrition) Meat contains a great deal of iron. Iron triggers free radicals and inflammation. I read that eating a lot of vegetables along with meat can offset some of the acidity of the meat.

Many farmers of conventionally raised cattle feed them grains (often corn to fatten them quickly for slaughter) that contain pesticides and may be genetically modified. Antibiotics and hormones are used to treat disease in cattle (which can be caused by the overcrowded conditions in which many cattle are raised.) I had read articles about elevated levels of hormones due to the lack of animal welfare and safety. I ate very little meat and when I did, I only ate free range, grass fed meat where it was stated that there was no use of hormones or of antibiotics.

Many people believe that charred meat can be carcinogenic. When meat is cooked at high temperatures it forms substances that cause cancer in some lab animals (according to the National Cancer Institute). Dr. Natalie E. Azar of NYU Medical Center advises against eating overly cooked meats since there is a chance they can increase the risk of colorectal, prostate and pancreatic cancer. (cancersupportindy.org).

There are many herbs that may be beneficial in the fight against cancer. According to *Planet Green* some are: **basil** – helps prevent cell damage from radiation, **ginger-** helps with nausea, **flat leaf parsley**- contains high levels of antioxidants, **mustard** –which may have anticancer properties, **turmeric** which contains **curcumin** which is an anti-inflammatory and may reduce the risk of cancer. (Dr. Baroody in his book "Alkalize or Die" – see bibliography, - states that **cayenne pepper** is a "miracle food" which stimulates the endocrine system.)

In an article published in the *Journal of Medicinal Foods* (June11, 2008) the following are listed as the top most potent herbs and spices: **ground cloves, ground cinnamon, ground Jamaican allspice, apple pie spice, ground** *oregano, pumpkin pie spice, marjoram, nutmeg, peppermint, sage, thyme, Himalayan salt and gourmet Italian spice.* Growing my own organic herbs, whenever possible, became a new interest.

I started using stainless steel pots and pans and high heat resistant nylon cooking utensils. I threw out my Teflon pans and utensils thinking that when they began to peel they couldn't be good for use. Where do all those little flaked off pieces go?

I bought glass storage containers. Plastic containers, even some marked BPA and PVC free are said to leach toxins when heated, scratched, old or washed numerous times in the dishwasher. I began storing most of our foods and drinks in glass containers. I used glass containers in the microwave for reheating. (I never cooked anything in the microwave since I had read that cooking foods in the microwave might change the molecular structure; and I was trying to eat as close to natural as possible.)

I began to notice the amount of cholesterol, saturated fats, transfats, etc. listed on food packages. I read about the recommended amount of grams appropriate for *my weight* and tried to follow the suggested amounts per day: total fat less than 65gr, saturated fat less than 20gr, cholesterol less than 300 gr

https://health.gov) sodium less than 2400ml (https// sodiumbreakup.heart.org), total carbohydrates 225-325gr (healthyeating.sfgate.com), fiber 25gr (WebMD) or more and protein being 46gr (WebMD). This is not easy to do but at least I had some guidelines. These numbers vary by age, activity level, caloric needs, etc.

Carbohydrates affect blood sugar levels. I knew that I needed to eat carbohydrates since they provide the body with energy. The foods with the most carbohydrates are: breads, cereals, crackers, grains, rice, pasta, potatoes, corn, peas, beans, fruits, fruit juices, milk, yogurt, sugary foods (candy, soda pop). Keeping the carbohydrates at 300 or less per day was almost impossible for me but I kept trying.

I had read that moderate exercise immediately after eating a high carbohydrate meal would help the body burn the carbohydrates instead of turning them into sugar – which cancer feeds on. Perhaps that is why people so often take a long walk after Thanksgiving dinner?

Sugar alcohols are a type of reduced calorie sweetener. They do not contain alcohol. Some sugar alcohols are: maltitol, mannitol, sorbitol, xylitol and isomalt. They are used in some sugar-free products.

Products that say sugar free may contain a lot of carbohydrates and/or calories so I would check the labels.

I became very aware of HFCS (high fructose corn syrup) in many of the things I ate. HFCS contains fructose and glucose. Chemically manufacturing HFCS produces fructose that is immediately absorbed by the liver. The liver then has the entire work of metabolizing this fructose. I was trying to help my liver function at its best so not eating foods containing HFCS became a goal. It was stated on the Mercola website (4/20/10) that "...glucose is used by every cell in your body and as such is far safer than the metabolic poison fructose."

Dr. Robert Ludwig is a Pediatric Endocrinologist. He gave a lecture in 2010 on *"Sugar: The Bitter Truth"* which is a YouTube viral video that I found of interest. He states that fructose gets turned into liver fat, which can prevent the liver from processing insulin properly.

I bought a good quality juicer. Juicing increases the amount of nutrients I could obtain from eating vegetables even though it decreases the amount of fiber. Many people use a Vitamix or other type of processer which keeps more nutrients (and fiber) than a juicer. Though I was missing a great deal of the fiber I had read that juices are easier to digest than the whole vegetable/fruit.

My thought was that if I couldn't pronounce the name

of an ingredient then I wouldn't eat it. That means avoiding as many foods as possible that contain artificial dyes and chemicals. I read the labels on everything. I never realized that the yogurt, which I thought was so good for me, had a lot of added sugar (with the exception of plain yogurt) as do many other processed foods.

I read the article *Is Sugar Toxic* by Gary Taubes in the New York Times Magazine April 17, 2011. The article discusses white granulated sugar (sucrose) and HFCS which are "effectively identical in their biological effects". It is stated in the article, "refined sugar is made up of molecules of the carbohydrate glucose bonded to molecules of the carbohydrate fructose – a 50-50 mixture of the two". The article goes on to state that "H.F.C.S. is 55% fructose and the remaining 45% nearly all glucose. The physiological effects are identical." Interestingly the author continues, "The fructose component of sugar and H.F.C.S. is metabolized primarily by the liver, while the glucose from sugar and starches is metabolized by every cell in the body. Consuming sugar (fructose and glucose) means more work for the liver than if you consumed the same number of calories of starch (glucose). He goes on to explain, "Insulin resistance is now considered the fundamental problem in obesity, heart disease, type II diabetes and perhaps many cancers." "Insulin resistance leads us to secrete more insulin which actually promotes tumor growth." It is further stated that Craig Thompson (President of Memorial Sloan-Kittering Cancer Center in New York) believes that "many pre-cancerous cells would never acquire the mutations that turn them into malignant tumors if they weren't being driven by insulin to take up more blood sugar and metabolize it". The article continues, "What researches call elevated insulin... appears to be a necessary step in many human cancers, particularly cancers like breast and colon cancer."

I try to eat low on the Glycemic Index list. Foods on the GI list are given a number from 1-100 depending upon their effect on blood sugar. Low for the Glycemic Index is 1-55; medium is 56-69 and high is 70-100. The Glycemic Index shows how quickly a food is digested.

More important to me is the Glycemic Load number given to a food. The GL list gives foods a number which is determined by the carbohydrate and the GI number. Low on the Glycemic Load list is 1-10; medium is 11-19 and high is 20+. A food may be high on the GI list but low on the GL list. Foods that are low on the GL list are processed more easily by the body than foods higher on the list therefore keeping the blood sugar levels more stable. Generally the more fiber a food has the better it will be for me since fiber helps to lower the GL number. There are many websites, books, articles that give the number on these lists for various foods.

I try to avoid genetically modified organisms (which according to Bill Freese at the Center for Food Safety are present in 60-70% of foods on US supermarket shelves). GMO's are made by a lab process that has been used to artificially insert genes into the DNA of a food or animal. These genes can come from bacteria, viruses, insects, animals or even humans. (gmo-awareness.com). The EWG has stated that about 90% of the corn crop grown in the US is genetically engineered. They also state that about 93% of the soybean crop grown in the US is genetically engineered. Unlike most industrialized countries the US does not require the labeling of foods that contain GMOs. The State of Vermont was the first state in the U.S. to pass legislation requiring labeling of foods containing GMO's - though not including meat, milk, restaurant items and alcohol - by July 1, 2016. The Grocery Manufacturers Association – more than 300 members including Starbucks, Green Mountain Coffee Roasters, Campbell Soups and Monsanto- began suing the State of Vermont about this legislation.) On July 29, 2016 President Obama signed Public Law 114-216 which overturned Vermont's labeling law and requires the federal government to set up its own standards for when a food must be labeled as biologically engineered (the Washington Times August 2, 2016).

Some companies voluntarily label their products "non-GMO" while others may say "Made without Genetically Modified Ingredients". Most genetically modified foods are made with corn, soybeans, canola and cottonseed.

I look for dairy products that are labeled "No rBGH"(bovine growth hormone) or "no rBST" (bovine somatotropin) or "artificial hormone-free".

I cannot begin to imagine eating transgenic fish (DNA has been altered using genetic engineering techniques). In 2015 the US Food and Drug Administration (FDA) approved the commercial production, sale and consumption of the AquAdvantage salmon. This is the first genetically modified animal to be approved for human consumption. (Wikipedia and U.S. Food & Drug Administration AquAdvantage Salmon Fact Sheet 12/21/15)

I buy foods that are certified organic, that are labeled "100% organic". Those labeled "organic" must contain at least 95% organic ingredients. Those that say "made with organic ingredients" are only required to have 70% of the ingredients be organic. (www.nsf.org).

88% of corn and 93% of soy grown in the U.S. is genetically modified. 94% of cottonseed is genetically engineered (used in vegetable oil, margarines, potato chips). 90% of the US canola crop is GE. Most GE food grown in the U.S. is "Roundup Ready" meaning it can withstand spraying of Monsanto's roundup pesticide and live, while weeds around it die. (www.huffpost.com Dec. 30, 2012).

I choose preserves, jams and jellies that are not made with corn syrup. Much of our corn is genetically modified. I try not to eat spreads made with corn syrup when other sweeteners can be added that are considered by many to be healthier.

Aspartame, NutraSweet and Equal are derived from

GMO's. See nonGMOShoppingGuide.com for more information.

The use of the Budwig Diet (cottage cheese and flaxseed oil) is said to increase the supply of oxygen to the cells. Since cancer does not like oxygen this was a diet I tried but didn't continue.

Omega 3 fatty acids are good fats that fight inflammation. The body cannot produce these on its own. The ratio of omega 3 to omega 6 is important. With our modern diet this ratio has become severely unbalanced with omega 6's far outweighing the omega 3's. Western diets are deficient in Omega-3 fatty acids and have excessive amounts of Omega-6 fatty acids. (www.ncbi.nlm.nih.gov)

I started my day by squeezing the juice of a lemon into filtered water. (I used a Brita Water Filter container and then poured that water into a glass container for storage for the day.) This lemon juice mixture is said to stimulate the digestive system.

It seemed as though everything that I liked was something I shouldn't be eating. I decided that I could manage without processed foods for a few months. I thought that 6 months should be enough time to cleanse my body.

The BEST book I found on nutrition is <u>Beating Cancer with Nutrition</u> by Patrick Quillin. There is a cd included which has most of the material contained in the book itself. If you read nothing else I would suggest that you read the first chapter.

I tried to stay away from anything – even organic – that was not grown/produced in the US or Canada. The whole <u>locavore</u> – eating food grown locally and as seasonally as possible – movement made perfect sense to me.

On the other side, Walter Willett, M.D. head of the department of nutrition at the Harvard School of Public Health is quoted in this same article, "If there is some benefit (from eating fruits and vegetables) it's pretty small and probably limited to specific cancers". (AARP Bulletin Dec.2012)

SUGGESTIONS I USED:

- During the meeting with the Herbalist I learned that many people believe that cancer feeds on sugar.
- I tried to avoid refined/regular table sugar and fructose found in many packaged goods.
- If I did eat a product containing sugar I tried to make sure the label said that it was made with "pure cane" sugar and not beet sugar (beets for beet sugar, which are different than the beets we eat, grow below ground).
- I began reading the labels on all packaged foods especially looking for how much added sugar each contained.
- I read that sugar consumption can depress the immune system for up to 6 hours. I tried to remember this fact whenever I ate something with added sugar.
- The American Heart Association recommends limiting added sugar to 6 teaspoons per day. (As stated in the January, 2013 issue of *Oprah Magazine* "Our actual intake is 22.2 teaspoons per day or about 3.2 cups week which is equivalent to 27 candy bars or 12 cans of soda in five days.")
- I read in numerous reports/articles that high fructose corn syrup (HFCS) was something I should try to avoid. So – I tried to avoid HFCS whenever possible. This turned out to be a huge task since HFCS seems to be in most packaged/highly processed foods (cookies, crackers, etc.)
- If HFCS is listed in the top ten ingredients of a packaged/processed food it is not a food I wanted to be eating.
- I began to avoid foods with labels which said: "modified food starch", "vegetable oil", "vegetable protein" (a soy

product), "rapeseed oil", "cottonseed oil", since they all sounded like something I did not want to ingest.

- Alice Bender, a registered dietitian with the American Institute for Cancer Research (AICR) is quoted in an article in *AARPBulletin*, December, 2012 "any level of alcohol increases the risk for breast cancer". The American Cancer Society recommends no more than one drink a day for women.
- I tried to eat organically raised fruits and vegetables from local sources. Since this was often difficult to do I decided that eating fruits and vegetables that are not organically raised is probably better than not eating them at all.
- I tried to only ate meat from animals that were grass fed and raised without antibiotics or any added hormones.
- I ate wild caught fish – from US and Canadian waters whenever possible.
- I read that fiber can offset some of the damaging properties of fructose so I increased the amount of fiber I eat.
- I read that fiber was crucial for gathering toxins and then helping to remove them from the body.
- Adults need 25-30 grams of fiber per day. Good sources of fiber are dried beans, oats, nuts, seeds, fruits and vegetables and whole grains used in breads/cereals/pastas.
- I chose to cook with the following pure oils: olive, sunflower and peanut since they come from crops where no GMO technology is used. (https://gmoanswers.com) I tried to be careful of the source since it has been found that there are producers who are not being truthful in their labeling of olive oil.

- Soybean oil, canola oil, cottonseed oil and corn oil are said to be almost entirely genetically engineered therefore I tried not to eat/use them.
- I found using the Mercola website (www.mercola.com) to be very helpful. There is a listing of grams of fructose found in various fruits.
- It is said that lactic acid (which is found in dairy products and also produced by cancer cells) feeds cancer cells so I tried to keep from eating dairy products as much as possible. I used organic almond milk, goat cheeses and coconut milk ice cream.
- I began using stainless steel for cooking and glass containers for storage.
- I learned that a cancerous mass often begins developing many years before it is discovered. A one millimeter cluster of cancerous cells typically contains about a million cells and on average takes about 6 years to get to this size. Generally a tumor cannot be detected until it reaches one millimeter in size. (drbenkim.com)

CHAPTER 15

Supplements

*"At the beginning of the cancer process, using supplements and
diet modification can help a great deal."
Dr. Stanislaw Burzynski quoted in the book Knockout*

Something I had never thought of before - Cancer is very big
business. It is shocking when you start either receiving bills or
see what your insurance company is being charged for various
drugs/tests/surgeries/biopsies/treatments.

Pharmaceutical companies spend years and billions
of dollars to have new drugs approved by the FDA. These
drugs can be incredibly helpful/life saving. Many of the
manufactured drugs also bring side effects that can be
uncomfortable at the very least.

Pharmaceutical companies cannot patent natural
occurring herbs. Companies producing these naturally
occurring "drugs" cannot afford to spend the billions of
dollars for research or marketing to prove the efficacy of their
supplements since there are no patent rights to drive up the
costs.

If you want to try using supplements which might help
with the side effects or to perhaps bolster your immune

system you'll have to do some research. Non-pharmaceuticals continue to be ignored by most conventional Western medical doctors since there is little education given in Western medical schools on this subject (www.drweil.com 2012).

As I stated earlier the Life Extension Foundation can give you more information about supplements than you can possibly absorb. Their suggestions, combined with information I found on various websites and from the Naturopath, enabled me to determine which supplements I wanted to start using prior to surgery. One could take many supplements but they can be expensive. I wanted to get as much benefit as possible for the least cost.

The first thing I learned is that the quality of supplements varies from manufacturer to manufacturer. I had to read each label to determine the content. Sometimes it takes multiple capsules of a supplement produced by one company to equal one made by another. I had to rely on the research of multiple groups to tell me which companies produced the highest quality products since there is no oversight or set standards.

BE SURE TO MENTION ANY MEDICATIONS, HERBS, SUPPLEMENTS YOU ARE TAKING TO YOUR HEALTH CARE PROVIDER; SOME CAN BE COUNTERPRODUCTIVE OR DECREASE THE EFFECTIVENESS OF SURGERIES, CHEMOTHERAPY, RADIATION, ETC.

Few have extensive research proving their effectiveness. It is best to meet with a health care professional such as a Naturopathic Physician to determine what is best for you.

Most of the information below is from the massive amount of literature of the Life Extension Organization, which appeared to be supported by numerous documented research studies. BUT – there is always a but. Colleen Doyle who is the director of nutrition and physical activity for the American Cancer Society stated in an article in *AARP Bulletin*,

December 2012, "Our bottom line message on supplements is that there's not enough evidence that they reduce cancer risk". This same article went on to state, "Studies have found that high levels of vitamins in pill form can sometimes increase cancer risk rather that reduce it."

BE AWARE that the list below is what I chose to take at various times. There are many possibilities.

1. *AHCC* - I had read that this is the number one cancer therapy in Japan. It is said to reduce the risk of hospital infections, fight the formation of abnormal cells and improve the immune system. It is a mushroom derivative.
2. *Bromelain* is reported, in many sources, to reduce inflammation. For years I read that inflammation in the body needs to be controlled to ward off arthritis, heart disease and cancer. Bromelain is also said to reduce the coating that keeps a tumor invisible to the immune system.
3. *Ginger* helps with nausea.
4. *Citrus Pectin* is said to decrease the ability of cancer cells to adhere to the lining of the blood vessels and to each other.
5. *Quercetin* is said to inhibit the growth of breast cancer cells, balance immune response, inhibit inflammation, support good glucose levels, reduce the stickiness of cells (thereby slowing metastasis) and competes with estrogen for binding sites (so diffuses the damaging effects of estrogen). One of the best sources of quercetin (which is said to be a potent anticancer supplement) is the white rind of citrus fruit. It is also found in apples, onions and grapes with skins - though grapes have a high sugar content. There is an interesting article in *Life Extension Magazine* September, 2014 p. 56-61 about Quercetin. On page

60 it is stated, "Quercetin has been shown to possess numerous anticancer properties...." On page 61 it is stated, "It was also demonstrated that quercetin binds to estrogen receptors just as tightly as Tamoxifen, the drug most used in breast cancer therapy."

6. *Green Tea Extract* is reported to help with healthy cell growth, to enhance immune function, and to be a powerful antioxidant. I like green tea but could not drink 5+cups per day which is the recommended amount. One capsule of green tea extract equals several cups.

7. *Vitamin D3* is said to inhibit mutant cell proliferation. I read that cancer cells are weak cells, because they are mutations; it is easier for the body to kill them off before they are able to clump together. For breast cancer patients it is said that Vitamin D3 levels should be near 80. (articles.mercola.com).

8. *Vitamin C* is an antioxidant. For years researchers have been suggesting that vitamin C is good for many physical problems.

9. *It is suggested that CoQ10* strengthens the mitochondria.

10. *Curcumin* is found in the spice Turmeric. Curcumin reportedly has strong anti-inflammatory and antioxidant properties. I read, in several sources, that this needs to be taken more than 2 hours after you take an Aromatase Inhibitor (a class of drugs often prescribed for long term use after the initial breast cancer treatments). There is controversy as to whether people using chemotherapy or taking an anti-coagulant should use curcumin.

11. *Milk thistle* contains silibium which is said to be a strong antioxidant and supports proper liver function.

12. *Melatonin* is a natural sleep aid to be taken before bedtime.

13. *Essiac Tea* is said to be an anticancer tea.

14. *Fish Oil* helps to balance the Omega 3's and 6's that are generally unbalanced due to our modern diet. Omega 3's are the good fats that help fight inflammation in the body. Fish oil is said to inhibit mutant cell growth. Since I also have problems with fibromyalgia the Naturopath suggested that it might help ease that problem also.

15. *Cod liver oil* is reported to help prevent metastasis of cancer cells by changing the stickiness of the cells and may reduce the growth of hormonally driven cancer.

16. *Cruciferous Vegetable Extract.* I found that I could not eat the amount of vegetables everyone was recommending so thought this might help.

17. I also took a high grade *multiple vitamin*. I made sure that the vitamin contained most of the following: Vitamins A, C, E, B12, B6, Vitamin D3, and Calcium. I read that in order to obtain all the vitamins and minerals one needs in a day multiple capsules are generally required.

18. Resveratrol is said to strengthen mitochondria, block estrogen and scavenge free radicals. Though Resveratrol is found in red wine it appears that the use of pesticides, when and what kind of grape is harvested all effect the amount found in the wine.

19. SAMe (S- adenosylmethionine) is reportedly helpful for depression and arthritis.

20. I tried Wobenzyme (which was quite expensive so I only used one bottle). This is a systemic enzyme (there are others including Nattokinase). It is said to reduce the stickiness of the blood cells (by thinning the blood). It is stated that anyone having a problem with clotting or who is taking a blood thinner SHOULD NOT take these. This is said to damage the protein coating of viruses which prevents the viruses from reproducing.

SUGGESTIONS I USED:

Before taking any supplements consult a trained health care professional. Supplements are "drugs". They can have unwanted interactions with other supplements and prescription drugs

- I found that capsules were much easier to swallow than tablets and less messy than powders.
- I began to be aware of how many capsules and servings were suggested per day.
- I began to notice the amounts of each ingredient listed on the label in order to determine which product to use. Some have far fewer amounts per serving than others.
- I did some research to find the manufacturer that I thought was best for the supplements I chose to take. There are numerous manufacturers with some having much better reputations for quality than others.
- I learned that fat-soluble nutrients, such as Vitamin D3, are better absorbed when taken with a meal containing some fat.
- I was told **NOT** to increase any supplement beyond the prescribed amount unless directed to do so by a healthcare professional. I was reminded again and again that these supplements are "drugs".
- In order to obtain the necessary amount of vitamins and minerals suggested by several different sources it appeared multiple capsules were necessary.
- I started using Cod Liver Oil since it was reported that it can help prevent metastasis of cancer cells by changing the stickiness of the cells and may reduce the growth of hormonally driven cancer.
- Systemic enzymes differ from digestive enzymes.
- I learned that systemic enzymes must be taken on an empty stomach.

CHAPTER 16

Decision Time

"There is always opportunity in crisis."
Old Chinese saying

Time was running out. I needed to make a decision. I had read many books, visited many, many websites, talked with my GYN, my PCP, my friends, doctors from Life Extensions, 3 surgeons, an Oncologist, a Complementary Medicine doctor, my massage therapist, and an herbalist so I had more information than I could comprehend. These people either said they couldn't tell me what to do or told me to have the surgery.

So much of the information I had read and heard mentioned "tumor load". The tumor was comprised of at least 1 million cells, some of which were dividing while I was making my decision. Having at least 1 million cells removed made sense to me. If some cells escaped there would be a lot fewer than the 1million+ for my body to deal with.

I read that there was an article in a recent issue of JAMA that stated that there was no difference in the outcome between surgeries using blue dye in addition to the nuclear injection and when the blue dye was not used. There were reported cases of people having allergic reactions to the blue dye. I didn't know if I would be allergic to the blue dye but why risk it? The surgeon at the small local hospital knew about the JAMA article and agreed that he would not need to use the blue dye. The surgeon at the large cancer hospital stated he would use the dye since that was the standard procedure there.

A friend told me about the <u>Oncotype DX</u> testing. This test is often used with women who have early stage breast cancer. I had asked both surgeons about having the testing done. The surgeon at the local hospital said, "of course" he would have the Oncotype DX testing done. The surgeon at the large cancer hospital said he would not order it.

The Oncotype DX Test is a diagnostic test that evaluates the activity of 21 genes in the tissue removed from the breast cancer site at the time of the surgery. It determines what your chances are of having breast cancer return and if you would benefit from chemotherapy. The test is used for women with early stage (stage 1 or 2) breast cancer that is estrogen positive and lymph node negative. The lower the score on the Oncotype DX Test the less likely that the breast cancer will respond to Tamoxifen chemotherapy or recur.

The next decision was about the removal of lymph nodes. I was very opposed to having any lymph nodes removed due to concerns about the impact it might have on my Lymphatic System (see Chapter 13). Surgeon #2 said that I could wait until the last minute to make that decision BUT if I chose not to have any removed he wouldn't have enough information to give me the best advice possible for what to do next. The surgeon at the large cancer hospital said that he HAD to remove the sentinel node/nodes.

Even though I had great respect for the people working at the hospital where I obtained the second opinion, the small local hospital seemed a better choice for me. Dr. Jimenez had a sense of humor, was willing to answer all my questions, was working in a hospital where there seemed to be less free floating anxiety, AND was willing to do what I asked.

I finally decided that, for me, it made sense to have the surgery and to have the sentinel node/nodes removed. Having it/them removed would give more information in order to make decisions about what to do next. I was comfortable with the decision even though it had taken a lot of effort and angst to make it.

SUGGESTIONS I USED:

- I used all the information I had obtained from various sources to make what I thought was the best decision for me. I decided that I needed to think that *I had made the best decision I could with the information I had at the time.*
- I asked my surgeon whether the Oncotype DX testing was something that would be helpful in making future decisions.
- I asked about the use of the blue dye.
- I asked about the nuclear injection.
- I asked what my breast would look like after the surgery.
- I asked for any suggestions that the doctor and nurses could give for before or after surgery care.
- I asked about recovery time.
- I asked about any limitations as far as exercise, baths, creams, etc.
- I asked about any restrictions on supplements, herbs, OTC (over the counter) medications, pharmaceuticals.

CHAPTER 17

Surgery

*"I needed patients' spirits to assist me in surgery and their
minds to be relaxed and in a state of trust before they went
into the operating room." Dr. Lori Arviso Alvord in her book
The Scalpel and the Silver Bear*

My surgeon had explained that he would do a lumpectomy
(may be called an <u>excisional biopsy</u>) by removing the tumor
and the tissue around it. He wanted to have "<u>clear margins</u>"
(cancer free breast tissue). When I asked how he would know
this he said that he had done over a 1,000 of these types of
operations and that he was confident that he could tell by "the
feel".

He told me that a pathologist would not be able to tell him
immediately if he had been able to get "clear margins" (often
said in place of "clean margins") so there was a possibility that
I would need another operation to get any tissue that might
still contain cancer cells. He stated that he had some concerns
about this tumor since it was so close to the chest wall.

He also said he would be removing at least one sentinel
node, though there might be more depending upon where the
radioactive material showed lymph had gone from the tumor.

I needed to trust that he would do his best and not remove any more nodes than he felt necessary; he knew how I had struggled with this decision.

Prior to surgery I was taking my supplements. **I made sure to inform the surgeon about these since even though they are "over the counter", they ARE drugs**. I was required to stop taking most of the supplements several days before the surgery. I was listening to cds by Peggy Huddleston for relaxation (see the Bibliography), eating well, trying to get enough sleep and having both massage and acupuncture treatments.

I asked the surgeon if he had any problem with me having my own music/cd playing in the operating room. I had read that there are studies showing people are aware of what is happening around them even though they are sedated/unconscious. I thought hearing my own music would be more helpful than hearing the talk in the operating room or the music someone else preferred. Dr. Jimenez asked that I label my cd player with my name but otherwise had no problem with the request.

I made sure that the music I wanted to listen to would loop for at least two hours since I had been told the operation would probably take about 1 ½hr. I wrote a note to the surgical team, which I pinned to my hospital gown, thanking them for taking good care of me. (I like to be thanked for my work so thought they might appreciate that; which one person commented she did.)

Prior to the surgery a radioactive material was injected into my breast. I was told that they would have a Geiger counter in the operating room to tell where the fluid had gone. This would tell which would be the first lymph node (Sentinel Node) that might have had cancer cells move into it from the tumor.

I informed the anesthesiologist that anesthesia had made me quite sick to my stomach in the past, so requested that he administer an anti –nausea drug. I also asked for an anti-anxiety drug and no morphine. I had read that morphine suppresses the immune system and that was something I was working hard to avoid.

Prior to going into surgery the nurses, who were assisting, came in to meet me. My surgeon and anesthesiologist both came in to talk with me.

After the surgery Dr. Jimenez met with my husband and told him that he thought he had been able to remove the entire tumor and had taken out seven lymph nodes. When my husband asked why he had removed so many Dr. Jimenez said that was where the radioactive substance had traveled.

SUGGESTIONS I USED:

- I used and continue to use the relaxation cd by Peggy Huddleston (see references).
- I asked about anti-nausea and antianxiety medications for the surgery.
- I thought I probably would not be able to raise my arm over my head after the surgery so had some front opening shirts available.
- I bought a sports' bra that zippered up the front which made me much more comfortable. I found this to be particularly helpful and often wore it at night time, too, long after the surgery.
- I purchased several nightgowns that would be easy to put on and take off without having to raise my arm too much.
- A small pillow was given to me by the Breast Care Specialist at the hospital prior to my surgery. The cover had been handmade by a breast cancer survivor who had attached a note of encouragement. This gift brought tears to my eyes. This was helpful in finding more comfortable ways to sleep.

- Another gift that touched me deeply was a small stone with the word courage carved into it. I carried that stone in my pocket for many months until I passed it on to another friend.
- I asked what they would be prescribing for pain medication for after the surgery. I had the prescription filled prior to the surgery so that the day of the surgery I could go straight home without stopping at a pharmacy.
- I bought a seatbelt cover so that there would be very little pressure across my chest. I still use the cover because I like the way it feels.
- I did not think to ask how many incisions the surgeon would need to make. I found two incisions when I awoke which was a surprise.
- I had some small cotton cloths available in case I had an incision where my bra might rub. These were helpful for many weeks after the surgery.

CHAPTER 18

Surgical Results

*"There may be scars on my chest,
but there need not be scars on my heart."*
Judy Kneece

Two weeks after the surgery Dr. Jimenez reviewed the pathology report with us. The report stated what each specimen consisted of i.e. sentinel node and/or tumor. Each node was identified and stated to have either "no tumor" or "tumor". The tumor itself was described with: the size, location, margin status, grade, tubal formation, number of mitoses, nuclear pleomorphism, BR Score, invasion status, Lymphocytic response, intraductal component, Histologic type, whether there was multifocal disease, lymphovascular invasion, and a review of the receptor analysis.

Out of all of that information what I heard was invasive cancer with no lymph node involvement.

I remembered that the tumor being under 2 cm was better than larger ones but also knew that small cancers can be fast growing and large cancers can be slow growing (www. breastcancer.org.). I read that the smaller the tumor the smaller the chance of lymph node involvement. Lymph node involvement changes the prognosis.

A <u>TNM classification</u> is the most often used method of breast cancer <u>staging</u>. Staging helps to determine the treatment method/s and prognosis. T stands for tumor size, N for the number of cancerous nodes and M for metastases -whether the cancer has spread to other areas of the body.

Dr. Jimenez told me that he was recommending an appointment be made with a <u>Radiation Oncologist</u>. He suggested a nearby radiology center so the appointment was made through his office.

I was also told that I would need to see a <u>Medical Oncologist</u>. The name of an Oncological group was given to me and an appointment made through Dr. Jimenez's office. I requested an appointment with a woman Oncologist. Dr. Jimenez said that it could take more than a week to receive the Oncotype DX test results. I had read that the results would indicate whether chemotherapy would be recommended.

I went home to try to decide if I wanted to keep those appointments and also to try to find out what all the words on the pathology report REALLY meant. I was quite sure I didn't want radiation and I was POSITIVE I didn't want chemotherapy.

SUGGESTIONS I USED:

- I took my co-patient to this appointment. I knew that this meeting was an especially important one for having my co-patient with me. I knew I would be given the results from the surgery. Whether the news was good or bad I wanted someone with me – someone to cheer or to hold my hand and listen to my fears whatever would happen.

- I was given a lot of information that seemed to be in a foreign language.
- I took very careful notes and asked my co-patient to do so, too. (I am usually pretty calm in a crisis so knew I would be able to listen reasonably well to what the surgeon would report but still wanted someone with me for moral support.)
- I requested a copy of the report to review as the surgeon was going over the results. I found this very helpful.
- I searched for the meaning of each unknown word on the report so I could ask questions at my next appointment.
- I asked for recommendations for what I should do next.
- I asked how much time I had to make decisions. I DID NOT make any decisions at that meeting. The surgeon's office staff made appointments for me with a Radiation Oncologist and a Medical Oncologist. I knew I could cancel either/both of the appointments if I decided to do so.
- After surgery adjuvant therapy is often used. It is used in addition to surgery which is considered to be the first phase. This can include chemotherapy and/or radiation therapy.
- I had read that margin width was a significant factor for recurrence so wanted to know exactly what that measurement was.
- I read about the Van Nuys Prognostic Classification which is said to be a way to determine whether there will be any gain from radiation treatments. In the end I did not contact these people to have the testing done.

CHAPTER 19

The Medical Oncologist

"Treat the person not the disease."
Sir William Osler.

I saw the Oncologist before seeing the Radiologist. I was thrilled to discover that the Oncologist worked out of Massachusetts General Hospital which is one of the premier hospitals in the world. She came to my local hospital one day a week. I was also thrilled to discover that she was about my age, was Harvard Medical School educated, had worked at NIH and that the walls of her office were covered with citations and awards. She obviously was very well educated and experienced. Best of all -I liked her the moment I met her!!

The report from the Oncotype DX testing was now available. For the Oncotype DX reporting there is a Low Risk Group, an Intermediate Risk Group and a High Risk Group. These groups give an average of what the percentage is for distant recurrence at ten years using Tamoxifen and for five years with and without the use of chemotherapy.

The Oncotype DX report placed me right in the middle of the Intermediate Risk Group. I was told that being in this group made the decision regarding chemotherapy quite difficult, since the researchers could not tell what the benefits might be. The Oncologist said that the decision was up to me. YEAH!! I easily decided that I would NOT have chemotherapy since the statistics didn't seem good enough to warrant all the potential problems; PLUS, I would be doing so many other things to change my lifestyle and, hopefully, strengthen my immune system. I felt pretty confident that my immune system would become strong and healthy; killing any cancer cells before they had a chance to grow into a mass/spread.

Dr. Browne reviewed the Pathology Report with me. This time I knew more of the words that we were discussing. She said that she would suggest that I start taking an Aromatase Inhibitor (an AI) on a daily basis. There were several that could be used, but given my situation and age, she would recommend Arimidex.

So began my next research. What were AI's? What did they do? What were the side effects?

SUGGESTIONS I USED:

- I did not understand much of the terminology being used but wanted to make sure that I understood what I had been told about clean margins and lymph node involvement
- I liked and trusted Dr. Browne, the Oncologist. She listened to my concerns and answered all of my questions.
- I knew I would be dealing with this person/office a number of times over the next five to ten years so knew I needed to be really comfortable with her, her nurse, the office staff, the location, the parking, and the easy availability for lab work, etc.
- I asked for copies of EVERY report even the ones just telling my height, weight, temperature, pulse

and blood pressure. I kept these in a section of my notebook so I could track any major changes.

- I made sure to receive a copy of the Oncotype DX report.
- One of the side effects of taking an Aromatase Inhibitor is bone loss. Dr. Browne suggested I take extra calcium, Vitamin D3 and exercise at least forty-five minutes per day.
- I asked about taking one of the bone strengthening prescription drugs I had seen advertised on TV. Dr. Browne said she would not recommend that. She did say that these were pharmaceuticals given to people who had more severe cases of cancer to help with this issue.
- I read that Arimedex – an AI – can affect cholesterol and the Immune System. Both of these were areas of concern for me.
- As time went on I began to feel depressed. When I mentioned this to Dr. Browne she stated that 98% of women with breast cancer become depressed at some point in the first year of treatment. She said she wished that I had told her sooner. She suggested therapy and/or an antidepressant. I did begin seeing a therapist but did not join a support group (though many people suggested I do so). I chose not to take an antidepressant though I knew many people who did and found it helpful.
- Now I noticed every lump/bump/swollen lymph node that appeared on/in my body thinking it was cancer. Dr. Browne said that I should be concerned about a lump which is hard and grows larger.
- Estrogen is produced by the body even after menopause. Fat cells produce estrogen. I thought losing a few extra pounds would mean less estrogen circulating in my body.

- Due to my many side effects from taking Arimidex, I was prescribed another drug – Aromasin, and then another, when Aromasin also produced unwanted side effects.

- I learned that the statistic for Arimidex working (in cases similar to mine) was 6-12%. I felt that with all the side effects perhaps another pharmaceutical might be better for me and my situation.

- I asked about statistics for each AI's possibility of working with my diagnosis. Though I generally try to ignore statistics I wanted to weigh the differences between the pharmaceuticals. I had to be very careful to note who was doing the research on these statistics, and who was paying for the research. I knew the old expression about the "fox in the hen house."

- When I saw the bills which were being sent to my insurance company for the AI prescription I was shocked (hundreds of dollars per month).

- I found it interesting to note that the annual sales of Arimidex are around $2.2 billion.

- I learned that there are many computer sites where people discuss their experiences using various pharmaceuticals. I knew I had to be very careful. Often people will talk about their problems but if they are not having any they do not comment.

CHAPTER 20

The Radiation Oncologist

"Selected nutritional supplements and a good diet can greatly reduce the side effects of conventional treatments."
Russell Blaylock, M.D.

Radiation Therapy (<u>Radiotherapy</u>) uses x-rays to stop cancer cells from growing and dividing if there are any cells remaining after surgery. This is done to reduce the risk of <u>recurrence</u> (having breast cancer again). In my case the treatments began several weeks after surgery since I had chosen not to have chemotherapy. I was scheduled for five days a week for four to six weeks with the last week or two being with higher levels (<u>booster</u>). This appeared to be the common course of treatment for my type of breast cancer.

Another option, (though not for me since I had so little breast tissue remaining), was <u>Accelerated Hypofractionated Whole-breast Radiation ("Canadian Radiation")</u>. This generally is five days a week for three weeks without the boost therapy, therefore decreasing the time and inconvenience involved.

I knew the treatments had some nasty side effects. Did having radiation treatments increase the statistics against recurrence enough for me to endure this? Were the side effects more than I wanted to deal with? Did radiation make sense, given my type of cancer?

Once I decided that I would have the traditional radiation treatments – and it took several visits to make the decision-I was "tattooed" so the machine would always be directed at exactly the same area. The tattooing entailed just 2 small blue dots, one in the middle of my chest and the other on the side. (I had not heard, though I imagine I was told, about the fact that the radiation would involve the area up to my collarbone and around my side.) I never understood why these markers had to be tattoos and not just some type of ink that would wear off over time. I thought about having the tattoos incorporated into a flower tattoo but never did since they are barely noticeable.

There was a session where they did a simulation of what would be happening on a daily basis. During this time I asked if I could take a picture of the machine. That was OK with everyone though they did ask why. I said I wanted to be familiar with the machine from an angle other than under it. I, also, wanted to name the machine. We were going to be spending so much time together and it was working to save my life so we should be friends. I named "my machine" and said "hello and thank you" to "her" during each visit. "Sunny" was not a particularly creative name but seemed to fit for my purposes.

I wanted to know exactly what would be happening so met with the medical dosimetrist (physicist trained in this area). He explained the calculations necessary for the radiation to target the site of my former tumor. I was concerned about where the radiation went – if it went in didn't it have to come out? – he showed me that, too. He said that I was fortunate as to the location of my tumor since only a small portion of one lung and a small portion of my liver would be involved. I asked what would happen to my thymus and lymph glands in the center of my body and was told that the radiation was so targeted that there was no need for extra precautions.

The possible side effects from radiation were stated to be: possible breast hardness, change in breast appearance, loss of volume, occasional discomfort, sensitivity, pale areola, lowered <u>Hemoglobin</u> levels (possible anemia) which can cause fatigue and the most common -- "sunburn".

I was introduced to the receptionist, billing staff, nurses, dietician, and to the "patient dog" (who brought so much calmness and love to the facility, always appearing happy to see me). I was shown where to change, (YEAH!! Real cloth gowns – it is the little things that make a difference), shown the room containing the machine and given my schedule.

The appointments were scheduled by date (five days a week for seven weeks) at the same time every day. The facility was quite flexible in the scheduling. If I needed to change the times there was no problem in doing so.

I signed the form stating that I had been told of all the possible side effects and understood what would be happening. So began the next phase.

I was surprised to find that the two technicians I dealt with initially were males. Though I was uncomfortable about this, especially with one being quite young, I managed and ultimately found them to be incredibly compassionate, caring, funny individuals. In this facility the techs rotated during the course of my treatment so some females worked with me, too. All of the techs were wonderful!!!! Though I was very happy when the treatments were completed I did miss seeing all of the people connected to the facility (and the treatment dog). I was given a certificate of completion at the end of the six plus weeks. I thought that was a nice way to end this phase of my long journey.

My appointments were for the same time every day so I began to meet people on the same schedule. This had positive and negative aspects. The positive was that we rapidly became friends as we were all fighting the same war. The negative was that I became saddened as I learned that several were losing the war.

There were days when I was so tired I could barely function. There were times when I sat at my kitchen table and was so exhausted that I just put my head on the table and cried. I was amazed, since while having radiation treatments I felt nothing. No one told me that being constantly tired is the number one complaint of cancer patients (and it continues long after the treatments have stopped). There are studies showing that a large number of people treated for cancer have much lower energy levels than most people for a long period of time after treatments have stopped.

SUGGESTIONS I USED:

- I asked about statistics for recurrence with and without radiation treatments. I was told that there was a study of patients eight years post treatment showing no recurrence in the same breast for 75% of people who received radiation and a 62% no recurrence in people who received no radiation.
- There are many facilities that offer radiation treatments (this is big business). I chose one where I felt comfortable, liked the staff, found parking/transportation to be convenient, was clean and cheery and not too far from my home.
- If someone is having difficulty with transportation contact can be made with the American Cancer Society. They have wonderful volunteers, many of whom have been on this same journey, who will give rides to and from appointments.
- I asked if I might be a good candidate for Accelerated Hypofractionated Whole-breast Radiation ("Canadian"

radiation) or any other types (such as receiving treatments while lying on my stomach.)

- I learned that exercise releases endorphins which might help with pain management and mood.
- I tried to exercise because I had heard it might help with the fatigue.
- I asked my Naturopath for suggestions for the use of particular herbs to help with the side effects of radiation. I made sure I cleared them with the radiologist before taking any.
- I asked about possible Lymphedema.
- I asked which deodorant, soaps, and shampoos they recommended during treatment.
- I asked which creams/lotions they recommended for the "sunburn" result of the treatments.
- I chose my own treatment for the "sunburn" but cleared it with the staff before beginning (i.e. using Aloe Vera plant)
- I had a shoulder issue on the side to be radiated. I knew I needed to keep my arm over my head for approximately 5 minutes during each treatment. I informed the technicians, in advance, so they could adjust the machine.
- It was suggested that I wear an old bra the day I was tattooed since the blue dye would remain on it for many washings.
- I asked which organs could possibly be affected by the radiation.
- My tumor had been very close to the chest wall so; it was felt that, radiation would be very helpful for me.
- I tried to remember that the techs and nurses at the radiation center were working to save my life. I took donuts and flowers at the time of my last visit and even stopped by several months later to take in another bouquet for the nurses' station (I thought they added

something cheery for the people walking by on their way to receive treatments and would add some color to the lives of the professionals who were working with very sick people all day long).

- I asked the best time of day to schedule my appointments. It was suggested that I schedule my appointments for as early in the day as possible since there would be less chance of being inconvenienced by problems with the machine, other people's appointment problems, doctors change in schedule, etc. This was a good suggestion since a doctor always had to be present when the machines were in use. The doctors often had early morning meetings in other facilities. They would then be detained making my early morning treatment later and causing backups as the day progressed.
- I decided that pool swimming was something I would not do knowing that chlorine levels are very high and that some consider chlorine a carcinogen.
- I have very sensitive skin and found that lake/pond swimming felt wonderful.
- I was told that I would never be able to have radiation on this breast again since the healthy cells had received as much radiation as they could safely handle.
- I experienced (and continue to experience) mild to moderate discomfort at times. I was told that this was due to the irritation of the nerves, swelling and scar tissue.
- I was concerned about information I read about women with breast cancer who were treated with radiation being more likely to develop heart problems in the future (Study: *Radiation for breast cancer can harm hearts September, 2013* article on Comcast). The article stated that "the chance of suffering a radiation-induced heart problem is fairly small". The conclusion

was "Don't forego radiation – whatever the cardiac risks they are outweighed by the cancer benefit".

- I asked about IMRT (<u>Intensity Modulated Radiation Therapy</u>). IMRT is said to pinpoint areas for radiation using a 3D method in order to avoid toxicity to the heart and lungs.
- I asked about the use of e-records to track radiation exposure over one's lifetime. This way a cumulative dose would be tracked so a person would know the risks and what tests would be safer in the future.
- I made "friends" with "my machine" by giving "her" a name.

CHAPTER 21

Complementary/Alternative

"Each patient carries his or her own doctor inside.
We are at our best when we give the doctor who resides within
each patient a chance to work."
Dr. Albert Schweitzer

Complementary and Alternative Medicine (CAM) practices do not rely on pharmaceutical drugs or surgery to treat illness. Complementary methods are used by many people in addition to conventional Western medical practices. Alternative methods are used by many in place of conventional Western medical practices.

Many believe that there is an imbalance between the body, mind and spirit which has allowed cancer cells to grow and multiply. I believed that I had some type of imbalance in my body but felt it was not my fault. I had lived my life as best I could up to this point. I had made choices that I thought were right for me given the information I had at the time. I KNEW I could not blame myself for this cancer but I could help myself to win the war against it returning.

I read about many different therapies and then chose several that made sense, sounded enjoyable and seemed as though I could do them without major effort. My life had now been taken over by cancer and there was just so much I could do in addition to trying to maintain my usual activities.

None of these therapies should be undertaken without the guidance of a Health Care Professional. No one should self-prescribe. Consult with your medical advisors to determine if any are contraindicated.

There are numerous complementary and/or alternative therapies (CAM) that one can try. The following is a listing of some that I explored:

Vitamin C therapy -- **NIH** has proven that high levels of intravenous vitamin C can kill cancer cells. I did not use this since it was too time consuming and I had to travel too far to receive the treatments.

Iscador -- is said to build up the immune system through injection of this mistletoe extract. This is used widely in Europe, especially Germany where it is paid for by the government for use by cancer patients. I was taught how to administer the shots to myself so I did not need to make the long trip to have the nurse give the injections. (This is not approved for use in the U.S.)

The *Traditional Chinese Medicine* (TCM) – This approach includes acupuncture and healing herbs. Acupuncture involves the use of very small needles said to open blocked pathways in the body. Traditional Chinese healing herbs should be used under the guidance of a trained practitioner. I did not find acupuncture to be helpful (I tried it for anxiety reduction) but know people who have found it to be very helpful for various conditions.

Aromatherapy -- involves inhaling the aromas of the oils of various plants. These oils can be made from the leaf, flower, stem, root, and/or bark of a plant. This is thought to enhance wellness in the body through improving thoughts/emotions. I found inhaling lavender aroma to be calming.

Ayurveda Medicine -- It has been used in India for centuries. The thought is that there are several basic body types. Once your body type is determined, foods, herbs, spices and various physical and mental practices are used for balance in the body. This is a whole system approach. I did consult with an Ayurveda Physician and used some of his suggestions and recipes.

Bioenergetics – This includes therapeutic touch, healing touch and Reiki among others. Often there are specially trained nurses in hospitals who might be available to work with patients. This is often called Energy Medicine. I had taken a Reiki course so did this for myself concentrating on my liver and my operated on breast.

Biofeedback -- It uses a specially designed machine to teach you how to control various bodily functions.

Breath Work -- This uses the breath to help control the mind, lessen stress and aid in the healing process. I found this very helpful especially during some of the tests and before surgery. I continue to use this often in my daily life.

Chelation Therapy -- It is said to draw toxins from the blood by using chelating substances administered via IV.

Chiropractic Therapy -- This is the manual adjustment of the spine so impulses can travel from the brain to various organs freely. I went to three different chiropractors before I found the right one for me. It certainly helped with my headaches. This was partially covered through my medical insurance.

Detoxification Therapy -- It uses various dietary changes to rid the body of adverse chemicals and toxins. The thought is to allow more energy for dealing with disease. I continue to use a modified version of detox with each change of season.

Guided Imagery – This practice uses CDs/tapes/teachers/ therapists to guide one's thoughts to fight disease in the body. In the case of cancer the idea is to picture, in your mind, what the cancer looks like and then picture something that will drive it out. I tried this method but found it did not work well for me. I have known people who have pictured their cancer as something to make friends with, others who have pictured themselves as warriors against an invading foe.

Herbal Medicine – This uses herbs/food and supplements to strengthen the body's immune system. As you can see from previous chapters this is what I chose to focus on. It gave me a sense of having some control and a feeling that I was doing something to help myself.

Homeopathy – This uses very small doses (tiny pills) of substances that cause symptoms which then encourage the body to produce what is needed to fight the problem.

Hyperthermia -- This is the use of warm water in various ways to strengthen the immune system. It is said that many "invaders" die when the body temperature is raised above 98.6. Hyperthermia includes the use of baths, hot packs, saunas, steam baths, etc. I found hot baths and hot packs to be helpful to me, though I had to take precautions not to have my operated on breast involved. Some believe that this is not appropriate for cancer patients.

Hypnosis -- It may help a person to relax, focus attention and concentrate. There are trained therapists who work with this technique. One can also learn self-hypnosis.

Journaling -- This practice consists of writing about feelings in order to lessen stress and to make some sense of what one may be feeling. This might be more helpful with the guidance of a psychotherapist or someone experienced in journaling.

Meditation -- This is often used to help with focusing and calming. This can be most effective when supported by a group or an experienced teacher. I chose to meditate alone.

Mindfulness-Based Stress Reduction Training (MBRT) – These techniques were developed by Jon Kabat-Zinn at UMassMedical Center in Worcester, Massachusetts. A report in *Mother Earth News* (September, 2014 by Linda B. White in the article *"An Invisible Network How Your Immune System Protects You"*) states, "In a 2008 Loyola University of Chicago study, women with early stage breast cancer who received MBSR Training had reduced levels of the stress hormone cortisol and improved natural killer cell activity and cytokine compared with women who did not receive the training". Natural killer cells attack problematic cells. Cytokine is a group of chemicals that help with cell communication.

Massage – This is the manipulation of the body to allow for relaxation, to decrease stress, and to release toxins. There are many different types of Massage Therapy used by trained therapists. I was very fortunate to find a very knowledgeable massage therapist who worked well with my body. Though I have had others work on my body I always return to this very talented woman with gratitude.

Prayer -- It is used by those who believe in a power/force inside or outside of themselves. Praying for yourself and being prayed for by a group can be very helpful/comforting.

Yoga -- There are many types of yoga from "hot" yoga, to laughter yoga, to traditional yoga using asanas (various postures) and breath work. The idea is to relieve stress and help with focusing as well as staying limber.

Crystals -- These are used by people who believe that there are certain crystals that can help with healing.

Magnets -- These are used by some people who believe that they help the body to heal itself.

SUGGESTIONS I USED:

- I talked with people who had experienced many of the Complementary/Alternative therapies to learn of their experiences.
- I Interviewed people trained in mind/body, whole/ body systems to determine who might be most helpful to me.
- I found the guide *Thinking about Complementary and Alternative Medicine* developed by NIH (National Institutes of Health 04-5541) to have good information and questions to ask about many of the techniques listed above.
- I used Complementary Therapies. I thought using both Western Medical offerings and Complementary Therapies would give me the best chances.
- I called my insurance company to see if any of these therapies were covered by my insurance. Sadly, most were not.
- I worked with a Nutritionist who was part of the radiation therapy facility for help with a detox diet and general nutrition.
- I bought myself a new pair of walking shoes and started to walk as often as possible. I listened to different types

of music on my iPod as I walked. I listened to stories on a playaway from the local library.

- I told any remaining cancer cells that I wanted them to leave my body.
- I used Reiki on myself focusing on both my liver and my operated on breast. (I had Level 1 Reiki training.)

CHAPTER 22

Spiritual

*"We must think over and over the kind of thoughts
we wish to dominate our lives."*
Henry David Thoreau

Even though there is no proven link between life style and the Immune System (www.health.harvard.edu) I felt there was. I also felt that there was a relationship between the mind and the body.

I am sure that physical, emotional and mental stress helped to weaken my Immune System so that cancer cells could clump together and cause the invasive cancer. I was working on the physical now but needed to work on the emotional and mental aspects.

I read that inharmonious thoughts are acid forming. (Dr. Caroline Leaf in "Who Switched Off My Brain" as quoted on www.platinumenergysystems.ca). Since I knew that I needed a more alkaline body I needed to focus on having more positive thoughts.

Doctor Baroody, in his book *"Alkalize or Die" (see references)*, thought that the vibrations that form color create a molecular impact within each cell. I surrounded myself in a rainbow of color to lift my spirits and to bring strength, relaxation, peace and joy. There is thought to be a purpose for each individual color.

Many believe we are vibrating beings. It is believed that the stronger the inner vibrations the healthier we are.

There are conflicting reports as to the effectiveness of eight weeks of training in MBSR (Mind Body Stress Reduction). Some report that people who practice MBSR have decreased signs of inflammation (Medscape Medical News, January 31, 2013). Inflammation appears to be part of many major illnesses.

There is an interesting section in Suzanne Sommers' book "Knockout" (see references) on the sympathetic and parasympathic nervous systems. It discusses the dominate types and which cancer each type is prone to.

QUESTIONS I ASKED MYSELF:

- What did I want to do with my "one wild and precious life" as Mary Oliver asks in her poem *The Summer Day*?
- What was my purpose for living?
- What did I believe about religion, spirituality, a Higher Power, a higher Self, God, the Source, Guides, whatever that SOMETHING is named?
- What is my passion?

CHAPTER 23

After Treatment

"I have noticed even people who claim everything is predestined, and that we can do nothing to change it look before they cross the road."
Stephen Hawking

Recovery takes time. This was the most important thing I had to remember after the treatments were completed. I had originally thought that when the treatments were finished I could resume my normal life. This was not true.

I had spent the last several months seeing doctors, nurses, radiation techs, having tests, surgery, and treatments. Now that the treatments were complete I was no longer seeing people on a daily basis who were focused on helping me to get well. I talked with people who had become depressed after all this attention was over. I thought, "That will never be me. I just want to get back to my regular life". I did not become depressed because of the lack of so many people focusing on me and my disease/treatment but I did learn that life will never be the same.

The issues I had to face included: which doctors did I need to continue to see and how often? Which tests did I need and how often? What could I do to lessen the fatigue and discomfort? Was there anything I could do to keep this cancer from coming back? Should I join a support group? Can/should I keep having complementary therapies?

Fatigue was my biggest problem during and after treatment. Almost a year after the end of my treatment I was still feeling tired much of the time. It was a relief to learn that this was normal.

What was happening to my brain? I used to have a good memory but now I was forgetting so many things. I learned that many survivors are dealing with memory/concentration problems. These problems may be due to the treatments, fatigue, pain, depression, stress, anger, "chemo brain", etc.

Lymphedema (swelling) is not uncommon in people who have been treated for breast cancer. I had to remember to be very kind to the arm on the treated side. I had been told not to have shots, blood tests, blood pressure taken, cuts, bites, extreme hot or cold on that side.

I took very good care of my teeth and saw my dentist regularly. I certainly did not want any kind of infection since I knew my body's immune system was weakened.

I started an exercise regimen. I had read (p. 5, *Nutrition Action Health Letter*, September, 2014 a quote by Heather Neilson, a researcher at Alberta Health Services in Calgary, Canada), "The evidence is growing that women have a lower risk of dying of breast cancer if they are more active after diagnosis".

Some of the possible side effects of cancer medications are weight gain, hot flashes and changes in sex life. I needed to be aware of these and take steps to make sure they did not impact my life. I researched all of these areas to determine what might be helpful to me. I learned that more than half of women treated long term for breast cancer encountered sexual problems. There are lubricants, exercises, sex therapists and counselors who can help.

I needed to continue to eat well and appropriately.

I dressed in layers, wore clothes that were "breathable", slept in a cool room.

Every discomfort, lump, and pain made me think I had cancer again. I learned that this, too, was very common. I found meditation and positive thinking helpful. "I've done all I can do. If cancer returns I'll have to deal with it then. I can't live my life worrying about it."

I got better at expressing my feelings. I did not blame myself for this cancer. I meditated, tried to find meaning in my life, investigated different religions and spirituality.

I made more of an effort to stay in touch with friends.

I finally made time to deal with making some advance legal directives. These are legal documents (some can be downloaded off the internet and signed in front of a notary so no lawyers are needed). These documents let people know your wishes in the event that you cannot do so yourself. I put the documents in a safe place where people would know how to find them i.e. a fire box (though made sure someone knew where the key was kept). Some of the basic documents are a living will, a durable power of attorney, a Health Care Proxy and a will. Single parents should make sure to spell out guardianship issues. Laws vary by state for many of these issues/documents.

SUGGESTIONS I USED:

- There is a website: www.caring4cancer.com where you can find survivor care plans.
- I found the following quote in an article in *Life Extensions Magazine* September, 2014 p.19 by Patrick l. Hill and Nicholas A. Turiano (reporting in Psychol. Sci. May 8, 2014), "Our findings point to the fact that finding a direction for life and setting overarching goals for what you want to achieve, can help you actually live longer, regardless of when you find your purpose".

CHAPTER 24

Statistics - which I try to Ignore

*"Why read statistics? Choose to live and do whatever is needed
to do that. If the statistics say only two people will survive -
Why shouldn't I be one of them? Don't tell me I am going to die.
Tell me I am going to live!"*
Lynn Walfish cancer survivor

Many people say that the statistics are about the same now as they were when President Nixon's "war on cancer" began in 1971. What has changed is earlier diagnosis. Another major change is that many women have stopped the use of hormones after menopause. "Breast cancer diagnoses climbed rapidly between 1980 and 1987, largely because of an increase in tumors detected by mammograms. The incidence rose again in the 1990's, thanks to the obesity epidemic and the widespread use of hormones after menopause. Between 2002 and 2003, diagnoses (especially of estrogen-positive tumors) dropped sharply after a major trial found that taking hormones raises the risk of breast cancer and many women stopped using them." (*Nutrition Action HealthLetter*, September, 2014 p.4)

The problem that I see is that billions of dollars are being spent on the treatment of cancer (which means HUGE profits for pharmaceutical companies and treatment centers) but not on prevention. NIH is doing some research on prevention but I think there needs to be a much greater effort in this area.

I didn't care about reading cancer statistics. I knew that one can make statistics come out the way the researchers want them to. Numbers can be manipulated, and misunderstood, due to poorly constructed research projects and varying points of view. But then, I thought, I'll see what they are saying but believe very little of it.

When I googled breast cancer I was directed to 14,200,000 sites. There are sites about studies done, there are sites with charts and graphs, there are sites about where to go for help, what to do, what to eat, what to avoid, etc., etc. It was overwhelming.

The numbers of breast cancer survivors seem to vary widely depending upon what is being read and who writes the articles/books. How could I compare the numbers of today, using improved early diagnosis, with the numbers in the early years when cancer was discovered only with the advanced growth of tumors?

The current numbers reported by many state that 1 in 8 women will be diagnosed with breast cancer in their lifetimes. (I remember that statistic being 1 in 9 at some point in the not too distant past.)

Over 200,000 women will be diagnosed with some form of breast cancer each year. (www.cdc.gov/cancer/breast/statistics/) About 85% of those women have no family history of breast cancer (BreastCancer.org).

The National Cancer Institute (JAMA July, 2013), as reported in the *New York Times* July 30, 2013 stated that some premalignant conditions like DCIS (Ductal Carcinoma in Situ), should be renamed. Many doctors agree that DCIS is not cancer. They suggest that such lesions be reclassified as IDLE (Indolent Lesions of Epithelial Origin) conditions.

Dr. Otis W. Brawley (CMO for The American Cancer

Society) says, "We need 21ˢᵗ century definitions of cancer instead of a 19ᵗʰ century definition of cancer, which is what we've been using."

"...early stage cancer requires a personalized approach to treatment" states Dr. Ernest Hawk, Vice President of Cancer Prevention of UTexas MD Anderson Cancer Center.

Many at the National Cancer Institute are concerned that "thousands are having needless treatments for lesions that are so slow growing that they are unlikely to ever cause harm."

Dr. Esserman at UC San Francisco stated, "DCIS is not cancer, so why are we calling it cancer".

Part of the problem is – how to determine which cases of DCIS will turn into an aggressive cancer and which won't. At this time there seems to be no way of determining which cancers are slow growing.

GLOSSARY

(The following definitions are from www.breastcancer.org, Breast Cancer Dictionary, cancer.gov/dictionary, Wikipedia, NCI Dictionary of Cancer, the Online Medical Dictionary as well as The Webster Dictionary)

A

Accelerated Hypo-fractionated Whole-Breast Radiation – radiation technique for early stage breast cancer using large daily doses for three to four weeks.

Acidic – tending to form an acid – a pH number less than 7.

Adjuvant Therapy – extra therapy to improve patients odds of surviving after the primary treatment is used (surgery is a primary treatment while chemotherapy and radiation are adjuvant therapies).

Alkaline – containing an alkali – a pH number greater than 7.

Allopathic - Another name for conventional, western medicine.

Alternative Medicine/Therapies – Practices used in **place of** mainstream western approaches.

Anaerobic – Not getting enough oxygen to the cells.

Ancillary Lymph Nodes – lymph nodes found under your arms.

Antioxidant- Decreases the free radicals found in the human body which cause cell damage.

Aromatase Inhibitor (AI) - Drugs that lower the amount of estrogen made in the body after menopause. This can slow or stop the growth of cancer that needs estrogen to grow. Arimidex, Femara and Aromasin are brand names of this type of drug. These are used to reduce the risk of systemic recurrence (recurrence elsewhere in the body – generally bone, lungs, brain).

Artificial Sweeteners – man made rather than occurring in nature.

Ayurveda – A form of alternative medicine used in India for centuries involving the entire body, mind and spirit.

B

Bacteria – plural of bacterium – unicellular microorganism which can cause disease.

Basement Membrane - This is the collagen surrounding the blood vessels. The stronger the basement membrane wall the more difficult for the cancer cell to enter the blood vessel and the less likely it is to metastasize. To strengthen collegian it has been suggested to decrease the omega 6 oils – corn, safflower, soybean, sunflower, peanut and canola. The use of zinc, grape seed extract (or pycnogenol) and curcumin have been suggested.

Benign - Has no signs of cancer. The growth of the cells in the tumor, cyst, lump, tissue, is under control. There is no spread to nearby tissue or to other parts of the body.

Biopsy – the removal of tissue to determine if it is or is not cancerous.

Boost - to increase.

Breast Cancer – abnormal cells in the breast that grow out of control which in turn produce more abnormal cells growing out of control.

Breast MRI – A test used for breast tissue that is very dense. About 1500 pictures are taken compared to 300-500 for a regular MRI.

BR Score – (Bloom-Richardson System) A system for grading breast cancer using a scale of 1-3 with one being the best.

C

Calcifications - Calcium that builds up in the tissue of the breast. It looks like grains of salt and can be seen on a mammogram. It cannot be found by touch.

Cancer – The name of diseases in which the body's cells become abnormal and divide out of control. Normal cells divide 50-70 times (www.quora.com) and then die. Cancer cells just keep dividing since they retain their long chromosomes by continually adding bits back on (www. sciencemuseum.org.uk). Normal cells "talk" with each other but cancer cells do not. Cancer is more common after the age of 65 since the DNA repair process becomes less efficient with age.

Cell Division – rapidly dividing cells indicate a faster tumor growth and a higher grade.

Centimeter - 2 1/2cm equal about 1 inch.

Clean (Clear) Margins – the tissue around the tumor that contains no cancer cells.

Complementary – These are practices that are not recognized as western medicine approaches. They can be used in conjunction with standard medical practices. The use of supplements, vitamins, herbs, massage therapy, acupuncture, meditation, spiritual healing, etc. may be suggested. These are used alongside NOT as a replacement for modern Western medicine.

Core/Cone Biopsy- This is the removal of a tissue sample with a hollow needle. The tissue is then looked at under the microscope to see if it's normal or abnormal.

Co-Patient – a term used by some people for the person who is the support person going through a medical situation with a patient.

COX2 – is an enzyme that causes inflammation and pain.

Cribriform – Invasive cribriform carcinoma is a type of cancer that is usually slow growing and non-invasive.

Cyst- A sac or capsule filled with fluid.

Cytologist – a specialist in looking at cells rather than tissue.

D

Detox - procedures used to counteract or destroy toxic material.

DCIS- Ductal Carcinoma in Situ - Abnormal breast cells that involve only the lining of a milk duct. These cells have not spread outside the duct into the normal surrounding breast tissue. This is also called ductal carcinoma in situ or intraductal carcinoma. Sometimes these are called precancers. Some authorities argue that this should be reclassified as a noncancerous condition. DCIS often does not progress to invasive breast cancer. (This was stated in *Well Being Journal* March/April 2012.) There are various subtypes of DCIS.

Diagnostic Mammogram – used when a woman has a breast symptom.

Diagnostic Procedures - A method used to see if a disease is present or not. It is also used to determine what kind of disease is present.

DNA – chromosomal constituent of living cell nuclei which determines individual hereditary characteristics.

Dosimetrist – a member of the Radiation Oncology Team. He/She calculates and prescribes doses of radiation so that healthy tissue and organs are not affected.

Duct - A tiny part of the body shaped like a tube or pipe. Body fluids pass through it – for example tear duct, bile duct, milk duct (which carries milk to the nipples).

Ductal Carcinoma – cancer found in a duct/ducts.

E

Encapsulated – Contained in a specific, localized area and surrounded by a thin layer of tissue.

ER – Estrogen receptors (which receive messages from hormones). These are special proteins that the estrogen hormone binds to. Breast cancer cells that are ER+ (ER positive) depend on estrogen to grow. Anti-estrogen hormonal therapy blocks the receptors or reduces the amount of estrogen that can attach to the receptors. As a result, the cancer cells may shrink or die. Cells that are ER- (ER negative) do not depend on estrogen to grow. Anti-estrogen hormonal therapy does not work with ER- cells.

Estrogen – A major female sex hormone. It is made in the ovaries before menopause and in the muscles and fat tissue after menopause. Estrogen also plays an important roll in males, especially as they age.

Equivocal – Of a doubtful or uncertain nature.

Excisional Biopsy – entire suspicious area is removed and examined.

F

False Negative – cancer is not found in the sample taken though it is cancerous.

Fibroadenoma – a knot of fibrous and mammary tissue that feels like a lump.

Fine Needle Biopsy- See Core Biopsy.

FISH (Florescence in Situ Hybridization) – A lab test that measures the amount of the HER2 (see below) gene in cells. It can be used to see if an invasive cancer has too many HER2 genes which are called HER2-positive (HER2+). This test can be used when the HER2 test is reported to be equivocal. Said to be more accurate than the HER/2 testing (www.breastcancer.org)

Fungi – plural of fungus - single or multi celled organism which can produce fruiting bodies such as yeasts and molds.

G

Gene – necessary for making new cells and controlling the growth and repair of cells.

Genetically modified (GMO – genetically modified organism) – Laboratory processes have artificially inserted genes into the DNA of a food or animal.

Grade – The grade of a tumor depends upon how abnormal the cancer cells look under a microscope and how fast the cancer cells are growing. The grade is thought to be directly related to the prognosis. Grade 1 cancer cells look a lot like normal cells. They are generally slow growing. Grade 3 cancer cells do not look like normal cells and are generally fast-growing.

GYN – variant – gynecology – medical doctor who specializes in female reproductive issues.

H

Hemoglobin – the oxygen-bearing, iron-containing protein in red blood cells.

HER2/neu– A gene that helps to control how cells grow, divide, and repair themselves. If there are too many receptors then the cancer tends to grow rapidly. (HER2 positive breast cancers tend to grow faster and are more likely to spread and come back compared to HER2 negative breast cancers www. breastcancer.org)

Herceptin – used in the treatment of abnormal HER2 genes.

Histologic Type – microscopic structure of animal and plant tissues.

Holistic – concerned with treating the whole.

Hormonal Therapy – used to help prevent recurrence. Therapy used to combat cancers that respond to estrogen and progesterone.

Hypnosis – an artificially induced sleeplike condition in which an individual is extremely responsive to suggestion made by a hypnotist.

Hypnotherapist (Hypnotist) – a person who is trained in the practice of hypnosis.

I

IDC- Infiltrating Ductal Carcinoma – A cancer that can invade other tissue. It begins in the milk duct but grows into the surrounding normal tissue inside the breast. It is the most common type of breast cancer. Various sources state 55% to 85% of breast cancers are IDC.

ILC (Invasive Lobular Carcinoma) – This is a cancer that starts in the milk glands and has grown into the surrounding tissue.

Image-Guided Biopsy – used if the lump cannot be felt. Computer mapping by mammogram or ultrasound is used.

Immune System – system in the human body that resists pathogens.

IMRT – Intensity Modulated Radiation Therapy – 3D method used to avoid radiation toxicity to organs.

Incisional Biopsy – a portion of the suspicious area is removed for examination.

Infiltrating Ductal Carcinoma – See IDC.

Infiltration- Infiltrating Cancer - Invasive - Cancer that has spread beyond the layer of tissue in which it started. It invades the normal surrounding tissues.

Integrative – bringing all parts together.

Integrative Medical Physician – a medical doctor who combines the use of standard, complementary and alternative medical practices.

Intraductal Carcinoma – see DCIS – Ductal Carcinoma in Situ.

Intraductal Component - within the duct.

Invasion Status – to spread into healthy tissue.

J

JAMA – Journal of the American Medical Association.

K

Ki-67 Test – a test showing how fast the cancer is growing.

L

Lesion – An area of abnormal tissue change.

Lobes – part of the breast that produces milk.

Local anesthesia – The area is numbed but the patient is awake.

Locavore – a person who is interested in food which is locally produced/grown.

Lumpectomy – Surgery to remove the cancer and a small amount of normal tissue around it – operating to remove the "lump" or tumor.

Lymph Nodes - part of the Lymphatic System. Lymph nodes try to trap cancer cells, toxins, debris before they/it moves into other parts of the body. In cancer it is best if the lymph node test result is negative (free of cancer cells). The more lymph nodes which have cancer cells found in them the more serious the cancer may be. Doctors look at the number of nodes involved and the amount of cancer in them to help make treatment decisions.

Lymphatic System – The system that carries nutrient rich lymphatic fluid to the cells and waste materials away from the cells to the circulatory system for expulsion from the body via the kidneys, lungs, skin, etc.

Lymphedema- Swelling caused by the accumulation of lymph fluid when the lymphatic system is damaged.

Lymphocytes - White blood cells. These cells fight infection.

Lymphovasular Invasion – blood vessels and lymphatic drainage that have cancer cells in them.

M

Malignant – Cancerous; a growth that tends to spread into nearby normal tissue and travel to other parts of the body.

Mammogram – An x-ray picture of the breast.

Margin Status/Width – The area of normal tissue around the edges of the tumor. This is sometimes called "clean" or "negative" or "clear" margins. The width of space between the cancer and normal tissue can vary from hospital to hospital with some requiring a cell width, others want 1 mm and others wanting 1 cm. At times more surgery is required if the surgeon has not removed all of the cancerous cells.

Massage Therapist – a person trained in rubbing/kneading parts of the body to aid circulation or relax the body.

Mastectomy – Surgery that removes the whole breast.

Medical Oncologist - A doctor who uses drugs to treat cancer.

Metastases – plural form of metastasis (see below)

Metastasis- The spread of cancer from where it started to another part of the body.

Metastatic cancer – When cancer has spread from the place where it started to another part/s of the body.

Microcalifications – tiny pieces of calcium found by x-ray.

Millimeter – (mm) equals 1/1000th of a meter. 1 Millimeter equals 0.0393 inch. 25.4 mm = one inch

Mitochondria – Create energy for the cells. It is involved with cell growth and death. In the human body the number varies by the type of tissue.

*Mitosis – The rate of cell division. In cancer situations the less the cells are dividing the better.

MRI – (Magnetic Resonance Image) - A test that looks at areas inside your body. Detailed pictures are made by a magnet linked to a computer. These are read by a radiologist.

Multifocal Disease – damage caused by disease occurring at multiple sites.

N

Natural Killer Cells (NK cells) - part of the Immune System – a type of lymphocyte (white blood cell) - defends against tumors and virus infected cells.

Naturopathic Physician/Doctor (ND) - A physician who practices naturopathic medicine. These doctors teach their patients to use diet, exercise and lifestyle changes to enhance their body's ability to fight disease.

Needle biopsy – A test that uses a hollow needle to remove tissue or fluid.

Non-invasive – cancer that stays where it started.

Nonmalignant - not cancerous.

*Nuclear pleomorphism – The change in cell size and uniformity from normal cells. If the cells are small and uniform they are given a score of 1.

O

Oncologist - A doctor who specializes in diagnosing and treating cancer.

Oncotype DX – a genomic test for early stage breast cancer used to analyze the activity of a group of genes that can affect how a cancer is likely to behave and respond to treatment.

P

Patient Navigator - a person hired by a hospital to assist patients with making appointments, obtaining needed information, etc.

Pathologist – A doctor who evaluates tissue or fluid taken from the body to see if it is normal or abnormal. If the tissue is abnormal he/she describes the nature and extent of the disease.

Pathology report – A report by a Pathologist that describes what was found in the fluid/tissue that was removed. There may be more than one report from one surgery.

PCP – Primary Care Physician.

Percutaneous Biopsy – the use of needles to remove samples through the skin.

Physician's Assistant (PA) – highly trained person who is part of a medical team.

Physicist – scientist who specializes in the interactions of matter and energy.

PR (Progesterone Receptor) – Breast cancer cells can have a special receptor (listen to signals from progesterone hormone) protein to which progesterone will attach. Breast cancer cells that are PR+ (PR positive) depend on the hormone progesterone to grow, and usually respond to hormonal therapy. PR- (Progesterone Receptor Negative) does not depend upon progesterone to grow.

Probiotics – live ("good") bacteria used to aid in digestion.

Progesterone – One of the hormones involved with fertility, menstruation and pregnancy.

Proliferation Rate –How fast cells reproduce.

Q

Quadrant – As the term is used in a pathology report it notes the tumor location. The breast area is divided into four parts (with the nipple being where the two lines intersect like a + sign). With the quadrants being "upper inner, upper outer, lower inner, lower outer". (At times the location is also noted as in looking at a clock i.e. 4 o'clock, etc.)

R

Radiation Therapy (radiation, radiotherapy) – The use of high-energy radiation from x-rays, gamma rays, neutrons and other sources to kill cancer cells and shrink tumors.

Radiation Oncologist - A doctor who uses radiation to treat cancer.

Receptor Analysis – evaluation of cell receptors.

Radiologist – A doctor who specializes in taking pictures of areas inside the body and determining what the pictures indicate. The pictures are made with x-rays, sound waves, or other types of energy. This specialist can also use imaging studies to guide procedures.

Recurrence – When the same cancer comes back after treatment. It can come back in the same place as the original or in a different part of the body.

S

Sentinel Node(s) – The first or first several lymph nodes away from a tumor. Generally this/these would be the first to have cancer cells in it/them from the site of the malignant tumor.

Sentinel Lymph Node Biopsy – This procedure was developed in the 1990's. These are the first nodes that cancer cells would go to from the tumor. If there are no cancer cells in the sentinel node/s then there is little likelihood that the cancer has spread to the axillary lymph nodes (those under the arm).

Stage – The range of a cancer, especially whether the disease has spread from the original site to other parts of the body.

Staging – This is based on the size of the tumor, the status of the lymph nodes and whether the cancer has spread beyond the breast. This information is used in determining the best treatment for each situation.

Stereotactic Biopsy - A method of taking a piece of tissue from an abnormality that is seen on an x-ray, sonogram, MRI, etc. but that cannot be felt. Since the abnormality cannot be felt, another way to locate it is needed. This is done using a computer and a three-dimensional scanning device to insert a needle in the correct location to perform the biopsy. Once the tissue is removed it is examined under a microscope to see if it is normal or abnormal.

Sonogram – use of ultrasound waves to create pictures of the inside of the body.

Surgeon – A doctor who removes or repairs a part of the body by operating.

T

3D Mammograms – x-ray pictures of the breast in 3 dimensions

Thymus – a gland like structure just behind the top of the breastbone that plays a part in resistance to disease in early childhood. The Thymus shrinks with age.

Titanium Clip – highly corrosion-resistant element with low weight and high strength that can be used as a marker.

TNM Classification – a widely used system for determining the extent of a person's cancer.

*Tubule Formation –The percentage of cancer composed of tubular structure. A score is given from 1 to 3. A score of 1 means slow growing.

---

* The scores of these 3 (Mitosis, Nuclear Pleomorphism, Tubule Formation) are added together to obtain a score of 3-9. A score of 3-5 is given a grade of 1 which has the best prognosis.

Tumor –An abnormal mass of tissue resulting from an overgrowth of cells. It may be benign or malignant.

Tumor Load – amount of cancer in the body.

U

Ultrasound – A machine which emits high frequency sound waves. A pattern of echoes which bounce off an abnormality is analyzed by computer.

V

Van Nuys Prognostic Classification – used to determine the aggressiveness of DCIS.

Virus – nucleic acid core surrounded by a protein coat - can only reproduce inside a living cell.

W

Well-differentiated – Cells generally appear normal and are not growing rapidly. (They look very similar to normal cells.)

Wire Localization – A small wire is placed in the breast. The wire is passed through a needle using x-rays as a guide so the surgeon can find the suspicious area.

REFERENCES

Baroody, Dr. Theodore. (2006) <u>Alkalize or Die</u>, Waynesville, North Carolina: Holographic Health Press.

Baylock, Russell, M.D. (2003) <u>Natural Strategies for Cancer Patients</u>, New York, New York: Kensington Publishing Corp.

Hass, Elson, MD. (2004) <u>The New Detox Diet</u>, Berkeley/ Toronto: Celestial Arts.

Huddleston, Peggy. (1996) <u>Prepare for Surgery, Heal Faster</u>, Cambridge, Massachusetts: Angel River Press: (includes – Instructional CD and Relaxation/Healing CD).

Kabat-Zinn, Jon. (1990) <u>Full Catastrophic Living</u>, 1540 Broadway, New York, New York: Dell Publishing.

Kneece, Judy, R.N. <u>Breast Cancer Treatment Handbook,</u> North Charleston, SC. 29418-2009: EduCareInc.com.

Quillin, Patrick. (2005) <u>Beating Cancer With Nutrition,</u> Carlsbad, CA 92013: Nutrition Times Press, Inc. Box 130789.

Segala, Melanie, Ed. (2003) <u>Prevention and Treatment,</u> P.O. Box 229120, Hollywood, Florida 33022: Life Extension Media.

Sharma, Kari, MD, et.al. (2002) <u>The Answer to Cancer</u>: New York, New York: Select Books, Inc.

Somers, Suzanne. (2009) <u>Knockout</u> New York, New York: Three Rivers Press.

Thomsom, Puja. (2007) <u>After Shock</u>. New Paltz, New York, 2007: Roots & Wings Publishing.

Trivieri & Anderson Editors. (1993) <u>Alternative Medicine the Definitive Guide</u> Berkeley, CA: Celestial Arts.

Weil, Andrew, M.D. (2004) <u>Natural Health, Natural Medicine</u>, 215 Park Avenue South, New York, New York 10003: Houghton Mifflin.

White, Linda, MD. <u>Mother Earth News</u>, (August-September 2014) "An Invisible Network: How Your Immune System Protects You", Topeka, KS 66609: Ogden Publications, Inc. 1503 SW 42nd St.

HELPFUL WEBSITES AND ORGANIZATIONS

Make sure to consult your physician before trying any new therapy. If you do choose to try something new MAKE SURE to inform your health care provider.

www.anh-usa.org ANH-USA (Alliance for Natural Health USA.) This organization is involved with an international organization supporting science and law to allow us all freedom of choice for healthcare. They have a weekly e-newsletter, *The Pulse of Natural Health*

www.breastcancer.org current cancer research

www.cancer.org (American Cancer Society) 1-800-227-2345

www.CANCER101.org

www.cancercenter.com Cancer Treatment Centers of America (diagnostic testing, latest treatment options, benefits of integrative therapies, other choices)

www.canceractive.com – Britain's #1 Complementary and Integrative cancer charity

www.cancertreatmentwatch.org

www.centerforfoodsafety.org

www.ewg.org The Environmental Working Group

www.healthwyze.org

www.lef.org Life Extensions

Laughter Therapy Groups – laughter affects the limbic system in positive ways.

www.mdanderson.org/ MD Anderson Center rated #1 Cancer Center in America by US News. Located in Houston, Texas

www.caringbridge.org MyCaringBridge (free) – a nonprofit website connecting family and friends to receive/send emails from/to the patient.

www.nationalbreastcancer.org National Breast Cancer Foundation

www.nsf.org – The Public Health and Safety Organization - independent certification organization

www.nutrition.org

www.pcrm.org Physicians Committee for Responsible Medicine

www.komen.org Susan G. Komen Foundation

www.breastthermography.com to find a Thermography Centers

www.cancer.gov

www.mercola.com

www.nongmoshoppingguide.com

www.mytreatmentdecision.com (Oncotype DX information)

www.greenmedinfo.com world's largest source of evidence-based natural medicine

www.nccih.nih.gov National Center for Complementary and Integrative Health which is part of NIH (National Institute for Health)

There is a very long list of books, videos, music and websites from the Leonard P. Zakim Center for Integrative Therapies at the Dana-Farber Cancer Institute in Boston, Massachusetts

There is a long listing of resources (including Books, Alternative Medicine Websites, Journals, how to contact some Alternative Physicians, and several Educational Groups and Support Groups) at the end of Suzanne Somers' book *Knockout.*

www.womenshealth.gov National Women's Health Information Center 1-800-944-9662

www.ingramcontent.com/pod-product-compliance
Lightning Source LLC
Chambersburg PA
CBHW032027290526
45786CB00011B/766